Charming
VILLAGE
SCENES
You Can
PAINT

Catherine Holman

NORTH LIGHT BOOKS

CINCINNATI, OHIO

I would like to dedicate this book to
my husband, Rick, and our children, Amber and Eric,
for always being there for me.

ABOUT THE AUTHOR

Catherine Holman has been painting since 1979. Although she began with oils, a six-week class in acrylics prompted her to switch mediums. Even before she had completed her acrylic class, she began teaching. Painting quaint villages and old, interesting buildings became her specialty.

A member of the Society of Decorative Painters, Catherine has taught at the national convention and travels throughout the United States and Canada to teach her style of painting to others. She is the author of three decorative painting books, a video and over one hundred project packets. She has been a contributor to several decorative painting magazines. Recently, four of her paintings have been released as limited edition prints and boxed notecard sets.

Catherine and her husband, Rick, reside in Excelsior Springs, Missouri, with their two children, Amber and Eric. Catherine's paintings sometimes include depictions of her family, as well as her two dogs, a Yorkie and a black Lab.

Charming Village Scenes You Can Paint. Copyright © 1999 by Catherine Holman. Manufactured in China. All rights reserved. The patterns and drawings in this book are for the personal use of the decorative painter. By permission of the author and publisher, they may be either hand-traced or photocopied to make single copies, but under no circumstances may they be resold or republished. It is permissible for the purchaser to paint the designs contained herein and sell them at fairs, bazaars and craft shows. No other part of this book may be reproduced in any form or by any electronic or mechanical means including information storage and retrieval systems without permission in writing from the publisher, except by a reviewer, who may quote brief passages in a review. Published by North Light Books, an imprint of F&W Publications, Inc., 1507 Dana Avenue, Cincinnati, Ohio 45207. (800) 289-0963. First edition.

Other fine North Light Books are available from your local bookstore, art supply store or direct from the publisher.

03 02 01 00 99   5 4 3 2 1

Library of Congress Cataloging-in-Publication Data

Holman, Catherine.
    Charming village scenes you can paint / by Catherine Holman.
        p.   cm.
    Includes index.
    ISBN 0-89134-901-4 (pbk. : alk. paper)
    1. Cities and towns in art.   2.   Acrylic painting—Technique.
I. Title.
ND1460.C57H66   1999
751.4′26—dc21   99-19350
                                                       CIP

Editors: Kathy Kipp and Jennifer Long
Production Editors: Michelle Howry and Christine Doyle
Production Coordinator: John Peavler
Designer: Mary Barnes Clark
Photography: Greg Grosse Photography, Cincinnati, Ohio

TABLE OF CONTENTS

GETTING STARTED

This book is for all those who have basic decorative painting skills, both beginners and more advanced students. Since the day I took my first acrylic lesson, I've always felt that anyone can learn to do decorative painting. Decorative artists love to share their talent and techniques, and generally teach in a step-by-step fashion. If you've never tried decorative painting, you'll find that it's very addictive. It seems to get in your blood, and you'll soon find there's not enough time in the world to paint all the things you dream of.

I generally only paint a project once because my mind is continually racing toward the next design. I've always loved teaching and sharing my love of painting with my students, and now, through this book, I'm able to share it with others around the world.

Brushes

Your brushes are your biggest investment. I generally use Loew Cornell brushes in the following sizes:

- Series 7300 nos. 10/0, 0, 1, 2, 4, 6, 10 and 16 flat shaders
- Series 7550 ³⁄-inch (1.9cm) wash brush
- Series 275 ³⁄-inch (1.9cm) mop brush
- Series 7000 no. 2 round
- Series 7350 no. 10/0 liner (short)
- Jackie Shaw no. 10/0 liner
- Assorted sizes of old, fuzzy flats for stippling

Loew Cornell also makes less expensive brushes than the ones listed above. If you haven't yet committed yourself to this hobby, you may prefer to start with a smaller investment. You can get by in the beginning with no. 2, no. 6 and no. 10 flat shaders, a no. 2 round and a 10/0 liner. The old, fuzzy flats used for stippling are hard for beginners to come by because they are old brushes that have generally been de-stroyed by basecoating. But believe me, you will soon find you have more old brushes than good ones.

The one thing I feel I must impress upon beginners: Acrylic paint dries just as fast in your brush as it does on your project. Rinse those brushes well and often! After rinsing your brush, blot it on a folded paper towel to see if any paint remains in the brush. Never load the paint over the ferrule of the brush (the metal part that connects the handle to the hairs). Once paint dries under the ferrule, the brush tends to get thick in the center and the hairs separate, making it impossible to paint with. You will have to dedicate the brush to stippling!

Brush Basin

I recommend using a brush basin with grids in the bottom to clean your brush. In the beginning, however, you can just use a couple of jars filled with water. You will use one jar for clean water and the other to rinse your brushes. One quick rule: Never leave your brush standing in the jar to soak. You will soon find you have a permanently bent brush.

The brush basins have grooves inside to rest your brush on and keep it from sliding to the bottom, and a divider in the center to separate your rinse water from your clean water.

Brush Holder

There are many different brush holders on the market today. A simple jar that is shorter than your brushes works fine. Be sure to store your brushes with the bristles up.

Paints

I use Delta Ceramcoat and DecoArt Americana acrylics in the 2-ounce (59ml) bottles. Bottled acrylics are thinner in consistency than tube acrylics and, I find, are easier for the beginner to work with.

Acrylic paints dry very quickly, but most mistakes can be fixed. Houses are a forgiving subject: Most buildings I paint are very old, so I can always use the excuse that the foundation was settling if something looks a little crooked. If there's something you're not happy with, such as a leaning porch post, paint a climbing rose bush going up it. If you're not happy with your shading or highlighting, simply paint over it with the base color and start again. You will soon learn there are many ways to fix a mistake that can lead to a piece that is more uniquely yours.

Miscellaneous Supplies

- Transparent grid ruler
- Scotch Magic Transparent Tape
- White and gray graphite paper
- Magic Rub eraser (to erase graphite lines)
- Bottle opener (to open paint lids)
- Q-Tips cotton swabs (great for quickly cleaning off mistakes)
- Viva paper towels
- Pad of palette paper for acrylic paints
- Tracing paper
- Designs From the Heart wood sealer
- Sponge roller
- 1-inch (2.5cm) sponge brush
- Small, stiff-bristle brush
- 400-grit black wet/dry sandpaper
- J.W. etc. Right-Step matte waterbase varnish
- Stylus
- Odorless turpentine (for oil paint)
- Burnt Umber oil paint
- Bubble wrap
- Styrofoam trays
- Palette knife
- DecoArt Americana Multi-Purpose Sealer DA17
- Krylon Matte Finish spray #1311
- Scissors
- Stain of your choice
- Rubbing alcohol

Surface Preparation

1. Seal all wood surfaces with Designs From the Heart wood sealer using a 1-inch (2.5cm) sponge brush and following the manufacturer's directions. Seal stoneware, bisque or unprimed tin with DecoArt Americana Multi-Purpose Sealer.
2. After the sealer has dried, sand wood with 400-grit black sandpaper. Remember, your painting will only be as good as your preparation.

Transferring the Pattern

1. Trace the design onto tracing paper with a fine-tip marker.
2. Position the pattern on your surface, and hold in place with clear tape.
3. Slide the gray or white graphite paper under your tracing paper. Go over the lines with a stylus, using light pressure. Too much pressure will groove the wood. Use white graphite on dark backgrounds and gray graphite on light backgrounds. Use a ruler when transferring straight lines.

Basecoating

This simply means to apply paint to an area to fill it in. Two to three coats are usually required, allowing each coat to dry completely before applying the next one. Make sure the basecoat is opaque (solid).

Floating

This is generally done with the flat shading brushes. Load the brush by wetting the bristles with *clean* water and gently blotting one side on two folded paper towels. Dip one corner of the brush into the paint, and blend back and forth with a sweeping motion in the same strip on your palette. The paint should be dark along one edge and fade to clear water on the other. If your paint seems to drag when you pull a stroke, you've probably blotted too much water out of your brush. If your float isn't clear on one side, you aren't blotting enough water out of your brush, or you're not using clean water. This simply takes practice, and we all know that practice makes perfect! All shading and highlighting are done with floated color.

Linework

To create fine linework, the paint must be thinned to an inklike consistency with water. Roll your brush between your fingers and out of the paint to twist the hairs to a point. Holding the brush straight up and down makes linework easier to control.

Wet, Float and Mop

This is an optional method, but one I think you'll enjoy once you've mastered it. To float, first dampen the area with water, apply the float, then lightly mop with a *dry* mop brush while the float is still wet. To do this you must keep your mop brush close at hand while painting. You won't be able to mop once the paint is dry, so work quickly. This will seem tricky at first, but you'll soon be surprised at the softness of these floats.

Back-to-Back Float

This technique is used to shade or highlight in the center of an area. With a little water, lightly dampen a much larger area than what you actually intend to float. Float in the center of the area, with the color fading to the right. Then, quickly float next to the first float with the color fading to the left. (The color side of the brush is always in the center.) Gently but quickly mop in all directions.

Stippling

Use a *dry*, old, fuzzy flat brush. Dip the tips of the bristles into the paint, and pounce on your palette in an up-and-down motion to tap out the excess paint. When there is very little paint left in the brush, you are ready to stipple. Test the effect on your palette first; it should look fuzzy. Stippling is done by lightly tapping the brush in an up-and-down motion to get a fuzzy effect. If your paint is "smushing" instead of stippling, or the hairs of your brush start to curl on the outer edges, you are tapping too hard. You should not be able to hear yourself stippling.

Project 1
TEA FOR ONE

Tea for One is exactly what it says. What a wonderful way to relax and enjoy your favorite cup of hot herbal tea and daydream about what you could paint next!

We all deserve our own quiet time, away from the stress of everyday duties, and now you can add this little tea pot and cup to your own special place of solitude.

MATERIALS

DecoArt Americana Acrylic Paints

Buttermilk DA3

Neutral Grey DA95

Antique Gold DA9

Winter Blue DA190

French Grey/ Blue DA98

Bright Green DA54

Mistletoe DA53

Rookwood Red DA97

Desert Sand DA7

DecoArt Americana Dazzling Metallics

Emperor's Gold DA148

Delta Ceramcoat Acrylic Paints

Black 02506

Mudstone 02488

Dark Forest Green 02096

Fjord Blue 02104

Burnt Sienna 02030

Santa Fe Rose 02496

Loew Cornell Brushes
- Series 7300 nos. 10/0, 0, 1, 2, 4, 6, 10 and 16 flat shaders
- Series 7550 ¾-inch (1.9cm) wash brush
- Series 275 ¾-inch (1.9cm) mop brush
- Series 7000 nos. 2 and 3 round
- Series 7350 no. 10/0 liner (short)
- Jackie Shaw no. 10/0 liner
- Old, fuzzy flats for stippling

Other Supplies
- DecoArt Americana Multi-Purpose Sealer DA17
- Tracing paper
- White and gray graphite paper
- Scotch Magic Transparent Tape
- J.W. etc. Right-Step matte waterbase varnish
- Magic Rub eraser
- Stylus
- Rubbing alcohol

Surface
The 7"-tall (18cm) *Tea for One* ceramic bisque teapot and cup are available from:
J. C.'s Pour 'N More
407 Main
P.O. Box 82
Spearville, KS 67876
(316) 385-2627

1 Prepare the Bisque

Wipe off any ceramic dust and clean the outside of the bisque with a soft cloth and rubbing alcohol. Apply one coat of DecoArt Americana Multi-Purpose Sealer to the outside of the tea-pot and cup. Allow to dry. Base the outside of the teapot, but not the lid, with Winter Blue. Trace the pattern onto a small piece of tracing paper. Tape the pattern to the teapot, slip a piece of white graphite under the trac-ing and use a stylus to transfer only the main lines of the building.

2 Stipple the Tree Foliage

Any tree foliage falling directly be-hind a building needs to be stippled be-fore the house is painted. It would be impossible to keep the paint off the house if stippling were done after the house was painted. For illustration pur-poses, I have transferred the pattern with gray graphite. Be sure you use white, because gray tends to dirty the light blue sky and can be difficult to re-move. Stipple heavily with the Dark Forest Green, lightly with Mistletoe and even more lightly with Bright Green. Always use a dry stipple brush.

This pattern may be hand-traced or photocopied for personal use only. This pattern appears at full size.

Stipple heavily with Dark Forest Green.

Stipple lightly with Mistletoe.

Stipple very lightly with Bright Green.

Basecoat the tea shoppe.

3 Basecoat the Tea Shoppe

Using a no. 1 flat, base the small roof on the gable with Black. Base the main area of the building and the chimneys with Rookwood Red. Use a no. 16 flat for the main area and a no. 2 flat for the chimneys. Base the siding on the gable with Mudstone on a no. 2 round. Base all the roof trim with Buttermilk, again using the no. 2 round. Base the porch step with Desert Sand on a no. 1 flat, then paint over the previous color on the lower half of the step with Mudstone, using a no. 10/0 liner.

4 Add Detail to the Tea Shoppe

Shade the top edge of the roof trim, the top of the Mudstone area on the gable and the top of the front step with Fjord Blue on a no. 2 flat. Paint a thin Black line on top of the Buttermilk roof trim to represent the main roof—use thinned paint and a no. 10/0 liner. To begin to add a little depth to the building, shade under the roof trim onto the brick area, under the chimney caps and the left side of the chimneys with a floated mixture of 1 part Rookwood Red + 1 part Black. Paint the

Begin adding detail to the tea shoppe.

brick mortar lines as shown on the pattern with thinned Mudstone and a no. 10/0 liner. Using Buttermilk, base the windows with a no. 4 flat, the flower boxes and the porch roof trim with a no. 1 flat, the doorway with a no. 10 flat and the porch posts with a no. 10/0 liner. Using Black, base the shutters with a no. 2 flat and the porch roof with a no. 10/0 flat.

5 Finish the Tea Shoppe
Base the inside area of all windows with Neutral Grey. Rather than transferring the pattern, paint the inside of the windows by using a brush the width of the area to be painted: Use a no. 1 flat on the upper windows and a no. 2 flat on the lower windows. Base the windows surrounding the door with a no. 10/0 flat. Shade the top and left side of the gray areas inside each window by floating on Black with a no. 2 flat. Outline the door with thinned Fjord Blue, using a no. 10/0 liner. Shade the top and left side of the panels on the door with Fjord Blue and a no. 1 flat. If this area is too tiny for you to float, simply outline the top and left side of each panel with thinned Fjord Blue and a no. 10/0 liner. Shade the top of the porch posts and the top of the door trim below the porch roof trim with Fjord Blue. Base the brass

kickplate at the bottom of the door with a no. 10/0 flat, and the door handle with a no. 10/0 liner, using Antique Gold. Shade the bottom of the kickplate and the left side of the door handle with Burnt Sienna. Highlight the kickplate and the handle with tiny dashes of thinned Buttermilk and a liner. Shade to the left of the handle with Fjord Blue. Add the gingerbread trim in the corners of the porch posts and the windowpane lines with thinned Buttermilk and a no. 10/0 liner. Paint the arched row of bricks above the windows with a no. 10/0 flat and Santa Fe Rose. Heavily stipple the bushes below the house and the flower foliage in the window boxes with Dark Forest Green on an old, fuzzy no. 2 flat. Stipple again lightly with Mistletoe. Dip one corner of the bristles of a fuzzy no. 0 flat in Rookwood Red and the other corner into Buttermilk (this

is a double load). Stipple carefully in one spot on your palette so the two colors start to blend in the center of the brush. Stipple in the individual flowers on top of the flower foliage and the bushes. Paint the vine up the right side of the building with Mistletoe and a no. 10/0 liner. Dampen the sky with a ¾-inch (1.9cm) wash brush and clean water (don't create puddles). Stipple the clouds with an old, fuzzy no. 4 flat and Buttermilk, then quickly and lightly mop the clouds in all directions to soften with a ¾-inch (1.9cm) mop brush. Mopping is a sweeping motion, just barely tickling the paint. If the clouds disappear, you're mopping too hard or you're using too much water. If the clouds don't do anything when you mop, you didn't mop quickly enough before they dried, or you didn't use enough water when you dampened the sky.

6 Paint the Sign

Base the tea shoppe sign with several coats of Buttermilk. Shade the sign with French Grey/Blue. Float the shading below the cup with a no. 2 flat and on the sides with a no. 4 flat. Paint the shading on the handle with thin paint and a no. 10/0 liner. Base the bracket with Black and highlight with French Grey/Blue. Paint the lettering with thinned Black. Whenever I paint lettering, I do the center letter or two first, then work outward. Paint the pinstripe on the cup and saucer with Rookwood Red, using a no. 10/0 liner.

Base the sign with Buttermilk.

Shade and add the bracket and lettering.

Add the highlights and trim.

Basecoat the lid with Rookwood Red. Paint the lettering with Mudstone, and stipple the wreath with Dark Forest Green.

Outline the letters with Emperor's Gold. Stipple the wreath lightly with Mistletoe.

7 Paint the Lid

Base the lid with Rookwood Red. It's easier to paint the lettering free-hand than to trace the pattern on. Just practice on a piece of tracing paper laid over the pattern. If you do decide to trace the pattern on, you will have to transfer one letter at a time using white graphite. (Gray graphite will show through the paint, and you'll have to go over your strokes more than once, which tends to make the letters grow.) Paint the lettering with Mudstone on a no. 2 flat, using shape-following strokes as in calligraphy. Outline slightly above and to the left of each section of every letter with thinned Emperor's Gold and a no. 10/0 liner. Stipple the wreath heavily around the edge of the lid with Dark Forest Green on an old, fuzzy no. 10 flat. Repeat the stippling lightly with Mistletoe, allowing the first color to show through. Paint the flowers as you did those on the teapot, using an old, fuzzy no. 2 flat double-loaded with Rookwood Red and Buttermilk.

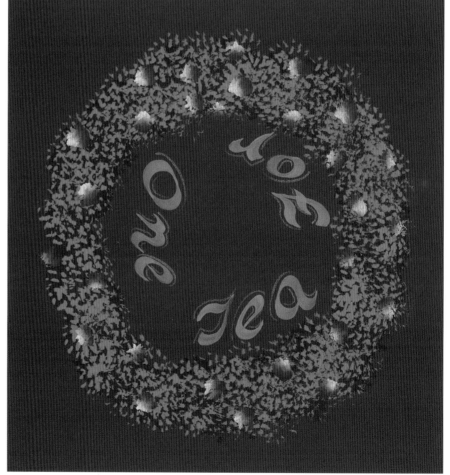

Add the flowers with Rookwood Red and Buttermilk.

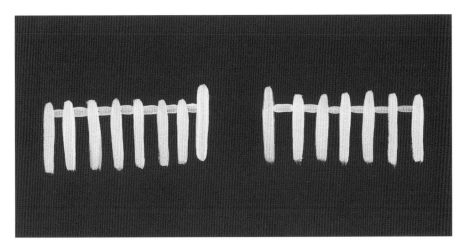

Paint the fence with Buttermilk.

8 Paint the Cup

Base the outside of the cup with Rookwood Red. Paint the fence at the top of the cup with Buttermilk on a no. 3 round, leaving an opening to line up with the step on the house. (Don't trace the pattern on; just eyeball it.) First paint the vertical boards, then the horizontal slats. You may have to apply two coats of paint. Shade the left side of each horizontal slat with a float of French Grey/Blue on a no. 2 flat. Stipple the bushes heavily with Dark Forest Green. Repeat the stippling lightly with Mistletoe. Paint the flowers with a fuzzy no. 0 flat double-loaded with Rookwood Red and Buttermilk.

9 Finish the Bisque

Remove any remaining graphite lines with a Magic Rub eraser and apply several coats of varnish. (J.W. etc. says its varnish is food safe.) This piece should be cleaned with a damp rag—do not soak in dishwater. Relax, put your feet up, and have a cup of tea!

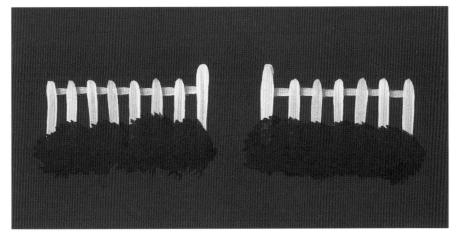

Shade with French Grey/Blue, and stipple the bushes with Dark Forest Green.

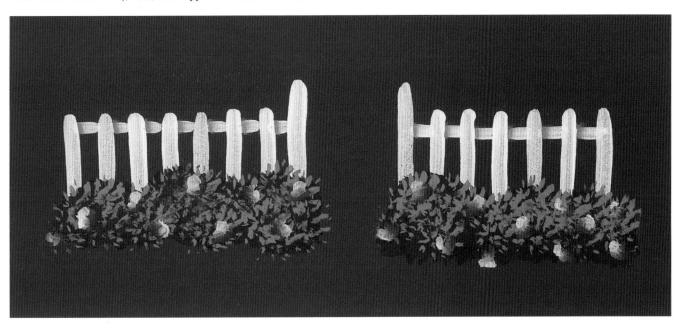

Stipple the bushes lightly with Mistletoe, and paint the flowers with a double load of Rookwood Red and Buttermilk.

Project 2
WINTER OIL LAMP

The twinkle of light coming from the windows in this evening snow scene makes you wonder who lives in these houses and what their quiet country lives are like. Smoke rising from the chimneys invites us in to sit by the fire and share stories of winters past.

This is a very simple project to paint. If you're intimidated by painting tiny details, simply enlarge the pattern to fit a larger lampshade or other surface of your choice.

MATERIALS

DecoArt
Americana
Acrylic
Paints

Buttermilk DA3	Moon Yellow DA7	Rookwood Red DA97	Black Plum DA172	Driftwood DA171	Milk Chocolate DA174

Dark Chocolate DA65	Slate Grey DA68	French Grey/ Blue DA98	Blue Mist DA178	Deep Midnight Blue DA166

Delta
Ceramcoat
Acrylic
Paints

Black 02506	White 02505	Burnt Sienna 02030

Loew Cornell Brushes
- Series 7300 nos. 10/0, 0, 1, 2, 4, 6, 10 and 16 flat shaders
- Series 7550 ¾-inch (1.9cm) wash brush
- Series 275 ¾-inch (1.9cm) mop brush
- Series 7000 no. 2 round
- Series 7350 no. 10/0 liner (short)
- Jackie Shaw no. 10/0 liner
- Small, old, fuzzy flats for stippling

Other Supplies
- Designs From the Heart wood sealer
- Americana Multi-Purpose Sealer DA17
- 1-inch (2.5cm) sponge brush
- 400-grit black wet/dry sandpaper
- Small, stiff-bristle brush
- Krylon Matte Finish spray #1311
- Magic Rub eraser
- Burnt Umber oil paint
- Odorless turpentine
- Tracing paper
- White and gray graphite paper
- Scotch Magic Transparent Tape
- J.W. etc Right-Step matte waterbase varnish
- Piece of bubble wrap

Surface
This wooden-based oil lamp with 7"-diameter (18cm) tin shade is available from:
Western Woodworks
1142 Olive Branch Lane
San Jose, CA 95120
voice mail and fax (408) 997-2356

First house

Barn

Second
house

Third
house

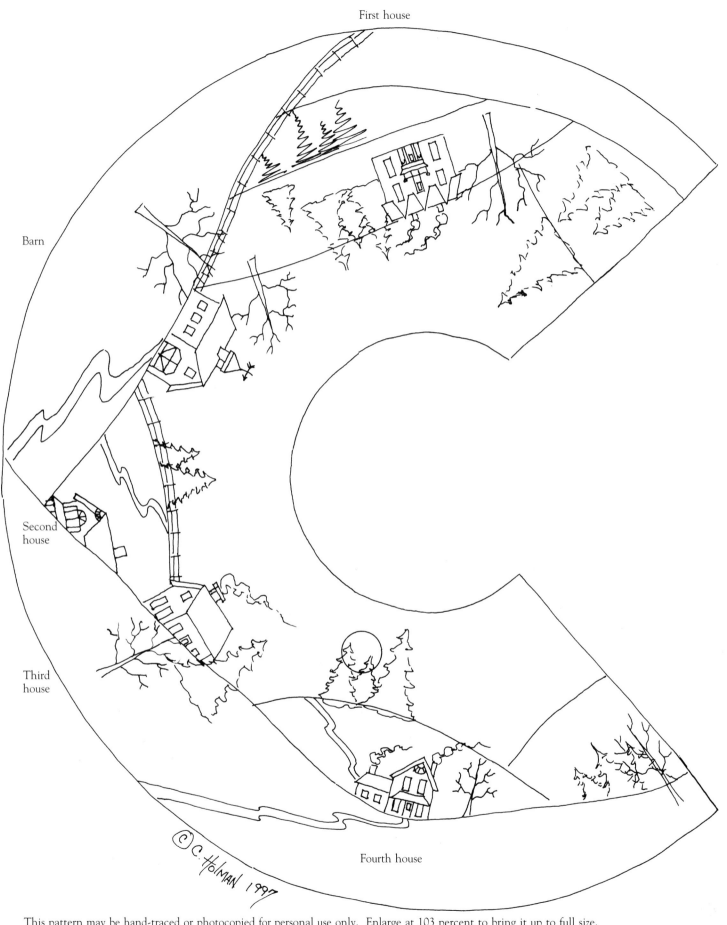

©C. Holman 1997

Fourth house

This pattern may be hand-traced or photocopied for personal use only. Enlarge at 103 percent to bring it up to full size.

◖ Charming Village Scenes You Can Paint ◗

1 Prepare the Surface

Apply wood sealer to the lantern base according to the directions on the bottle. When dry, sand with 400-grit sandpaper. Wash the shade thoroughly with warm, soapy water. Sand the tin lightly to roughen the surface. Apply DecoArt Americana Multi-Purpose Sealer to the shade, inside and out, with a ¾-inch (1.9cm) wash brush. Base the entire outside of the shade with Deep Midnight Blue, again using a ¾-inch (1.9cm) wash brush. Apply four to five coats, until opaque. This will give the shade a smooth, even surface.

2 Transfer the Pattern and Base the Ground Area

Trace the pattern onto tracing paper. Cut out the tracing along the outer edge. Shape the tracing into a funnel and tape the two edges together. Slip this onto your shade and position carefully, then tape to secure. Slip white graphite paper under the tracing, and transfer the pattern for the hills over the Deep Midnight Blue. Base the ground area with a no. 16 flat and French Grey/Blue.

3 Highlight the Hills and Pond

Wet the top of the hills and above the pond, then highlight by floating a mixture of 2 parts White + 1 part French Grey/Blue. Mop to soften. Base the pond with a mixture of 1 part French Grey/Blue + 1 part Deep Midnight Blue on a no. 6 flat. Shade the pond by floating Deep Midnight Blue at the bottom. Highlight the top of the pond with a floated mixture of 2 parts White + 1 part French Grey/Blue.

Base the entire outside of the shade with Deep Midnight Blue.

Base the ground with French Grey/Blue.

Highlight the hills and pond with floats of color.

4 Base the First House

Transfer the pattern for the main areas of the house, excluding windows, doors and other details. Base the main area of the house with Driftwood using a no. 4 flat, base the roof with Black and a no. 1 flat and base the chimneys with Rookwood Red using a no. 10/0 flat.

5 Base the Barn

Using a no. 4 flat, base the right end of the barn with Rookwood Red and the left side of the barn with Black Plum. With a no. 10/0 flat, base the right side of the cupola on the roof with Buttermilk and the left side of the cupola with Driftwood. Base the roofs with Black and a no. 1 flat.

First house.

Barn.

Second house.

6 Base the Second House
Base the main area of the house with Blue Mist on a no. 4 flat, the roofs with Black on a no. 1 flat and the chimney with Rookwood Red on a no. 10/0 flat.

7 Base the Third House
Using a no. 4 flat, base the right side of the house with Milk Chocolate and the left end with Dark Chocolate. Base the right side of the chimney with Rookwood Red and the left side with Black Plum, using a no. 10/0 flat. Base the roof with Black on a no. 1 flat.

8 Base the Fourth House
Base the main area of the house with Slate Grey on a no. 4 flat, the chimneys with Rookwood Red on a no. 10/0 flat and the roofs with Black on a no. 1 flat.

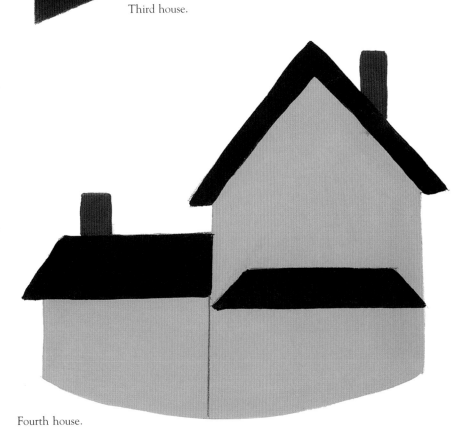

Third house.

Fourth house.

9 Add Detail to the First House

Using a no. 4 or no. 6 flat, shade under the roof with a mixture of 2 parts Dark Chocolate + 1 part Driftwood. Shade the chimney with a mixture of 1 part Black Plum + 1 part Black on a no. 2 flat. Base the door with Black. Base all windows with Moon Yellow on a no. 10/0 flat. Float the shading on the top and left side of all the windows with Burnt Sienna, using a no. 2 flat. Paint the pane lines in all the windows with thinned Dark Chocolate on a no. 10/0 liner. With thinned Buttermilk on a no. 10/0 liner, paint the trim along the roof and above the door, outline the windows and paint all gingerbread trim and porch posts. Shade the roof trim above the door with Slate Grey. Outline above this roof trim and paint the shutters with Black.

First house.

10 Detail the Barn

Shade under the roof with a mixture of 1 part Black Plum + 1 part Black on a no. 4 or no. 6 flat. Base the windows with Black on a no. 10/0 flat. With a no. 10/0 liner, outline the windows and door and paint the trim along the roof with thinned Buttermilk. Still using a no. 10/0 liner, paint the weather vane with thinned Black and add a line down the center of the barn door.

Barn.

11 Detail the Second House

Shade under the roof with a mixture of 3 parts Blue Mist + 1 part Black. Shade the chimney with a mixture of 1 part Black Plum + 1 part Black. Base both windows with Moon Yellow on a no. 10/0 flat. Float the shading on the top and left side of the windows with Burnt Sienna, using a no. 2 flat. Paint the pane lines in the windows with thinned Dark Chocolate on a no. 10/0 liner. With thinned Buttermilk on a no. 10/0 liner, paint the trim along the roof and above the door, outline the windows and paint all gingerbread trim and porch posts. Paint the shutters Black.

12 Detail the Third House

Shade under the roof with a mixture of 1 part Dark Chocolate + 1 part Black. Shade the chimney with a mixture of 1 part Black Plum + 1 part Black on a no. 2 flat. Base all windows with Moon Yellow on a no. 10/0 flat. Float the shading on the top and left side of all the windows with Burnt Sienna, using a no. 2 flat. Paint the pane lines in all the windows with thinned Dark Chocolate on a no. 10/0 liner. With thinned Buttermilk on a no. 10/0 liner, paint the trim along the roof and sides and outline the windows.

13 Detail the Fourth House

Shade under the roofs with a mixture of 1 part Slate Grey + 1 part Black. Shade the chimney with a mixture of 1 part Black Plum + 1 part Black on a no. 2 flat. Base the door with Black. Base all windows with Moon Yellow on a no. 10/0 flat. Float the shading on the top and left side of all the windows with Burnt Sienna, using a no. 2 flat. Paint the pane lines in all the windows with thinned Dark Chocolate on a no. 10/0 liner. With thinned Buttermilk on a no. 10/0 liner, paint the trim along the roof and above the door, outline the windows and paint all gingerbread trim.

Second house.

Third house.

Fourth house.

14 Paint the Moon and Stipple the Evergreen Trees

Base the moon with Buttermilk. Shade the left side of the moon with French Grey/Blue. Stipple the evergreen trees heavily (until solid) with Black on an old, fuzzy no. 0 flat. Try to form a few branches on the sides of the trees. Now lightly stipple the front trees with a mixture of 1 part White + 1 part Deep Midnight Blue, working from top to bottom. Allow some of the Black to show through, and keep a shadow between each tree. Stipple the back tree last, stippling very lightly at the bottom to leave a shadow. Now you can begin to see a slight separation between the individual trees. Next, create a lighter value of the same mix by adding more White. Stipple the trees again to add more depth, again keeping the shadows between the trees and allowing the first two colors to show through. Where the moon would shine on the top of the trees, add touches of White with a liner. If your trees don't look quite right, simply start over by stippling them again with Black and repeating with the snow colors.

Stipple with Black.

The biggest problem most of my students have with evergreen trees is the need to loosen up and not stipple such neat little triangles. It looks as if someone came along with a hedge trimmer on these trees.

Stipple with White + Deep Midnight Blue.

Stipple with a lighter value of the previous mix.

Add touches of White where the moonlight hits the trees.

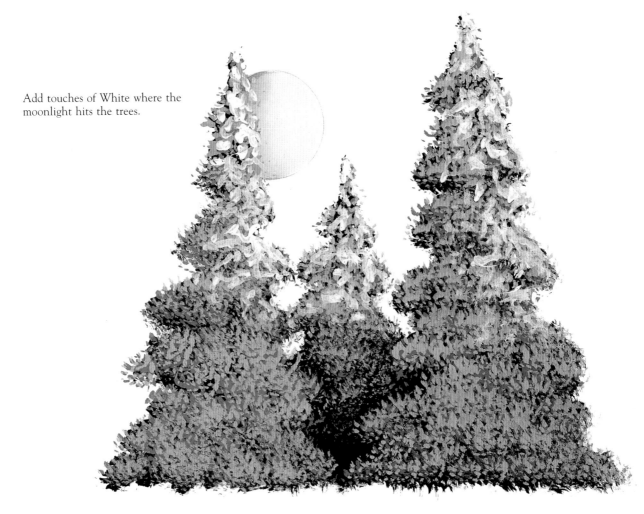

15 Paint the Reflections in the Pond and Stipple in Bushes

Dampen the pond with a little water, scribble a reflection for the evergreen trees with Black and a no. 2 round and quickly mop with a horizontal stroke to blur the reflection. Allow to dry, then dampen again with a little water and use a liner to quickly scribble a mix of 1 part White + 1 part Deep Midnight Blue on top of the Black. Again mop horizontally to blur. Using the same technique, apply White with a liner to the top of the tree reflections.

The house reflection in the pond is done in the same manner. Dampen the pond with a little water, base the main area of the house with Driftwood and mop to blur. Allow to dry, then dampen, base the roof with Black and mop. When dry, dampen again and add the windows with Moon Yellow, the door with Black and the roof trim above the lower door with Buttermilk, mopping in between each step. Using a no. 10/0 liner and thinned Buttermilk, add some shine lines at the top of the reflections.

Stipple bushes below the first house, starting heavily with Black, then lightly with a mix of 1 part White + 1 part Deep Midnight Blue. Repeat with a lighter value of this mix (adding White) and once again with White at the top of the bushes.

The tree reflections are done with a no. 2 round and Black, scribbled in a tornado pattern. Always dampen, apply reflection and mop to blur. Work small areas of the reflections at a time so you have time to mop before an area dries.

Add snow colors to the trees and mop. Do not transfer a pattern for the house reflection. It doesn't have to be perfect. The bushes are stippled in the same manner as you did the trees.

16 Add the Fences

Base the fences with a no. 10/0 liner and Dark Chocolate. Highlight the right side of each vertical post with Milk Chocolate. Add some snow on the fence with a liner and a mixture of 2 parts thinned White + 1 part French Grey/Blue.

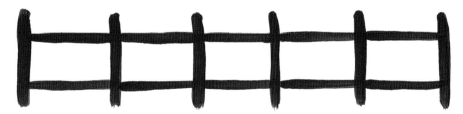

Paint the fences with Dark Chocolate.

Highlight with Milk Chocolate.

17 Add the Remaining Trees

Base all remaining trees with a mixture of 1 part Dark Chocolate + 1 part Black. Add some snow on the branches with a thinned mix of 1 part White + 1 part French Grey/Blue and a liner.

Paint the trees with Dark Chocolate + Black.

Add snow with White + French Grey/Blue.

18 Paint the Chimney Smoke

Dampen the sky above the chimneys with a little water. Float the smoke with a small flat brush and Slate Grey, then quickly mop to soften. On the two houses in the valleys, highlight the smoke above the chimneys with a little Buttermilk.

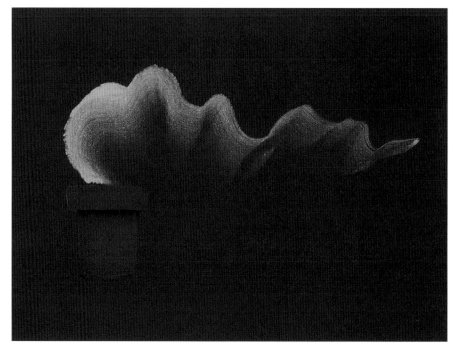

Float the chimney smoke with Slate Grey.

Mop to soften.

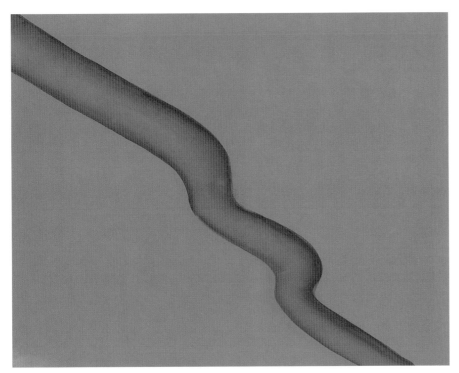

Shade the roads with Deep Midnight Blue.

19 Paint the Roads

Shade the inside of the roads by floating Deep Midnight Blue with a no. 4 flat. To highlight the outside of the roads, wet, float and mop with a mixture of 2 parts White + 1 part French Grey/Blue on a no. 16 flat. Repeat this highlight two to three times to get the right intensity. Also highlight below the trees with this mix.

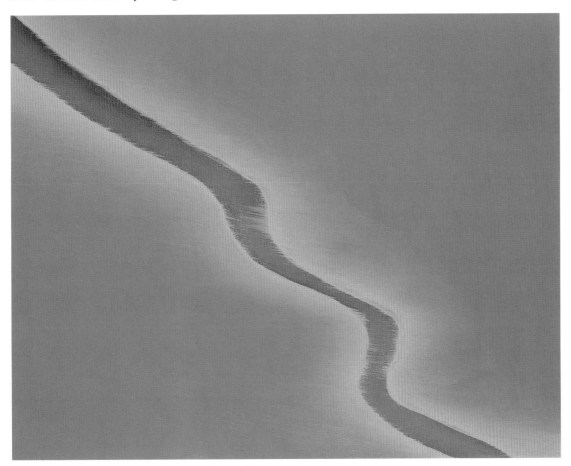

Highlight the roads with White + French Grey/Blue.

The finished scene.

20 Finish the Scene

Add reflections on the ground from some of the windows with a wash of Moon Yellow. To create falling snow over the entire scene, load a small, stiff bristle brush (a toothbrush works fine) with thinned White. Run your finger over the end of the bristles. (Test this on your palette first to be sure you have a fine spattering.) If desired, you can varnish the shade before spattering so that if you're not satisfied with the results, you can clean it off and try again.

21 Finish the Lamp

Base the inside of the shade and the upper and lower rims with Rookwood Red. Also paint the wooden base of the lamp with Rookwood Red. Spray the lamp base with two to three light coats of Krylon Matte Finish spray. Apply a mix of Burnt Umber oil paint and turpentine to the base of the lamp with a sponge brush. The mix should be dark but easy to spread. Carefully wrap a piece of bubble wrap around the base (you need a piece big enough to go all the way around the base) and press gently. Do not move the bubble wrap while it's touching the base. Gently remove the bubble wrap, and allow to dry thoroughly.

If you're not happy with the design, remain calm—oil paint is very slow to dry. Simply repeat the procedure by brushing over the antiquing with your sponge brush and reapplying the bubble wrap until you're happy with the design. Allow to dry one to two weeks. Remove any remaining graphite with an eraser, then apply two to three coats of varnish.

Paint the lamp base with Rookwood Red.

Apply Burnt Umber antiquing with a sponge brush.

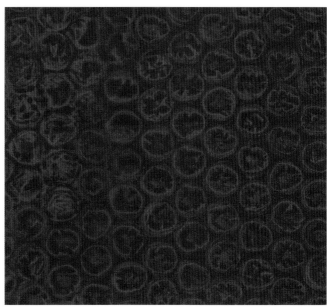

Lay bubble wrap over the antiquing and press evenly. Popped bubbles won't leave an imprint.

Project 3
VILLAGE BOWL

I couldn't wait to design the little village scene to paint on the wide rim of this unusual bowl. At first I was going to paint the design in the center of the bowl, but the rim kept beckoning to me. I also realized that if I painted the design in the center, it would be covered if I decided to use the bowl. This piece would look great filled with apples or pinecones in the center of your dining room or kitchen table. It makes a great centerpiece!

MATERIALS

DecoArt Americana Acrylic Paints					
Buttermilk DA3	Eggshell DA153	Slate Grey DA68	Antique Gold DA9	Terra Cotta DA62	Ice Blue DA135
Blue Mist DA178	French Grey/ Blue DA98	Bright Green DA54	Mistletoe DA53	Rookwood Red DA97	Black Plum DA172
Khaki Tan DA173	Light Cinnamon DA114	Dark Chocolate DA65	Neutral Grey DA95		

Delta Ceramcoat Acrylic Paints					
White 02505	Black 02506	Mudstone 02488	Dark Forest Green 02096	Wedgwood Green 02070	Fjord Blue 02104
Salem Green 02099	Santa Fe Rose 02496	Adobe Red 02046			

Materials List continued on page 34

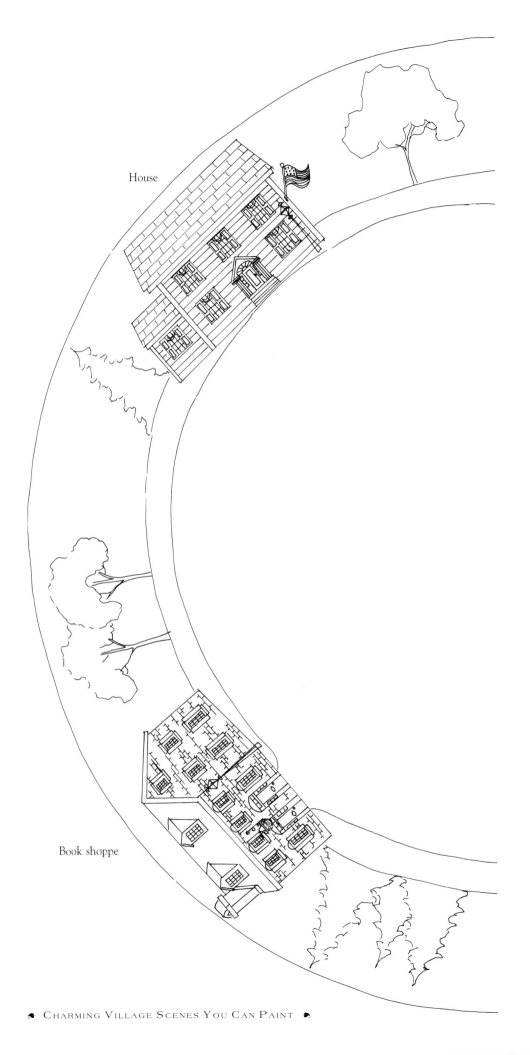

House

Book shoppe

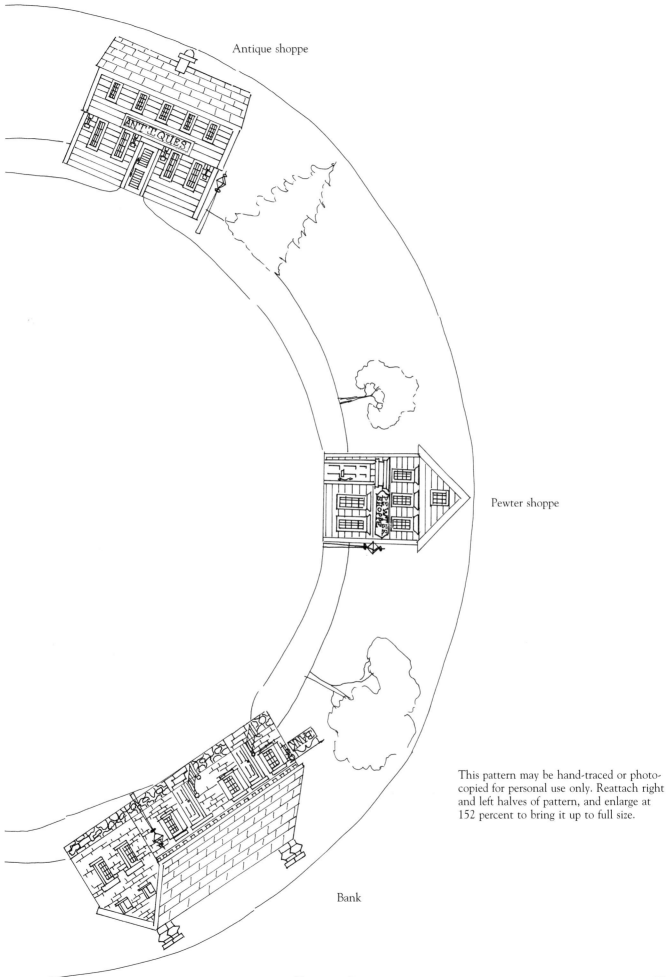

Antique shoppe

Pewter shoppe

This pattern may be hand-traced or photo-copied for personal use only. Reattach right and left halves of pattern, and enlarge at 152 percent to bring it up to full size.

Bank

Loew Cornell Brushes
- Series 7300 nos. 10/0, 0, 1, 2, 4, 6, 10 and 16 flat shaders
- Series 7550 ¾-inch (1.9cm) wash brush
- Series 275 ¾-inch (1.9cm) mop brush
- Series 7000 no. 2 round
- Series 7350 no. 10/0 liner (short)
- Jackie Shaw no. 10/0 liner
- Old, fuzzy flats for stippling

Other Supplies
- 1-inch (2.5cm) sponge brush
- Krylon Matte Finish spray #1311
- Burnt Umber oil paint
- Odorless turpentine
- Tracing paper
- Scissors
- White and gray graphite paper
- Scotch Magic Transparent Tape
- J.W. etc. Right-Step matte waterbase varnish
- Bubble wrap
- Magic Rub eraser
- Paper towel

Surface
This 14″-diameter (36cm) steel bowl is available from:
Barb Watson
P.O. Box 1467
Moreno Valley, CA 92556
(909) 653-3780

1 Prepare the Bowl
This bowl comes preprimed. Simply base the wide part of the rim (approximately 2½″ [6cm] wide) from the sidewalk up with Ice Blue, using a ¾-inch (1.9cm) wash brush. Trace your pattern onto tracing paper, and cut out each individual building. Tape the tracings of the buildings to the rim of the bowl, spacing them evenly. Transfer the patterns for the buildings onto the bowl very lightly with gray graphite paper. Don't transfer any windows, doors or trim.

2 Base the Pewter Shoppe
Base the main area of the building with Santa Fe Rose, using a no. 10 flat.

3 Base the Bank
Base the left side of the brick area and the left side of the chimneys with Rookwood Red. Base the right side of the building and chimneys with Black Plum. Use a no. 2 flat for the chimneys and a no. 10 flat for the main areas. Base the roof with Slate Grey on a no. 10 flat. On the left side of the building, base the roof trim and the foundation with Mudstone. Base the roof trim and foundation on the right side of the building with a mixture of 1 part Mudstone + 1 part Fjord Blue. Use a no. 2 round for the roof trim and a no. 4 flat for the foundation.

Pewter shoppe.

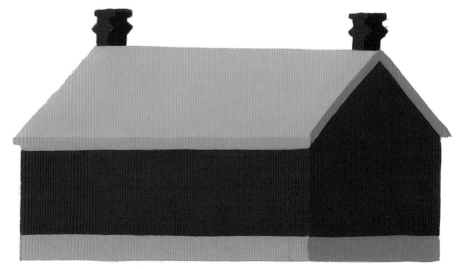

Bank.

4 Base the Book Shoppe

Base the front of the building and the front of the chimney with Terra Cotta. Base the right side of the chimney and building with Light Cinnamon. Use a no. 10 flat for the main areas and a no. 2 flat for the chimney. Base the roof with Neutral Grey on a no. 4 flat. Base the roof trim on the front of the building and the front of the gables with Buttermilk on a no. 2 round. Base the roof trim on the right side of the building and the right side of the gables with Eggshell, again using a no. 2 round. Paint the flashing at the bottom of the chimney on the front with a mixture of 1 part Buttermilk + 1 part Neutral Grey on a no. 2 round. Add a little more Neutral Grey to the mix, and base the flashing at the bottom of the chimney on the right side. Base the gable roofs with 1 part Neutral Grey + 1 part Black on a no. 2 flat.

5 Base the House

Base the main area of the house with Salem Green on a no. 10 flat. Base the roof with Neutral Grey on a no. 10 flat and the roof trim with Mudstone on a no. 2 round.

6 Base the Antique Shoppe

Base the main area of the building with Khaki Tan on a no. 10 flat. Base the roof with Light Cinnamon on a no. 10 flat, and the chimney with Rookwood Red on a no. 2 flat. Using a no. 10/0 liner and thinned Black, paint the arch at the top of the chimney.

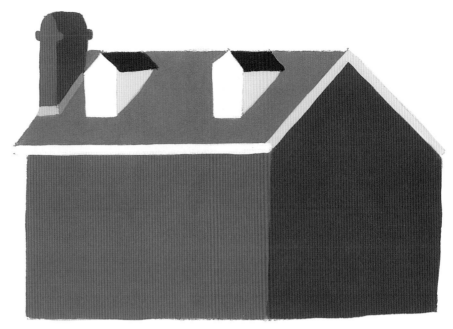

Book shoppe.

House.

Antique shoppe.

7 Begin to Detail the Pewter Shoppe

Float Light Cinnamon shading below the roof trim and next to the trim on the edges of the building with a no. 6 flat. Using thinned Light Cinnamon, paint the lap siding lines, holding the brush perpendicular to the surface and using only the tip of the brush. Transfer the pattern for the windows, door and sign. Base the windows and door with a mixture of 2 parts Santa Fe Rose + 1 part Adobe Red on a no. 4 flat. Use a no. 10/0 liner to outline the windows and the door with thinned Dark Chocolate. Base the sign with Dark Chocolate on a no. 2 flat.

8 Finish the Pewter Shoppe

Base the inside area of all windows with Black on a no. 2 flat. Paint a Black line along the upper edge of the roof. Do all liner work with thinned paint on a no. 10/0 liner. Float all shading using a no. 4 flat in the larger areas and a no. 2 flat in the smaller areas. Shade the top and both ends of the sign with Black. Paint the pane lines in the windows with a thinned mix of 2 parts Santa Fe Rose + 1 part Adobe Red (also used to base the window area). Shade below the roof trim again, below the ledges on the window trim and the ledges above the doorway with Dark Chocolate. Shade the door with Salem Green at the top and both sides. Shade once again with a mixture of 1 part Salem Green + 1 part Black. Shade the top and left side of each panel on the door with this mix. Paint the mail slot on the door, the door handle and the lettering on the sign with Antique Gold. Shade the gold areas with thinned Light Cinnamon and a liner brush. When shading the lettering, apply just a little here and there; this tones down the lettering and gives a brass appearance. Highlight these same areas with tiny flecks of thinned Buttermilk. Shade to the right of the door handle with a mix of 1 part Blue Mist + 1 part Black. Outline the sign with thinned Blue Mist.

Add shading and base the main details of the pewter shoppe.

Complete the details.

9 Begin to Detail the Bank

With a mixture of 1 part Black Plum + 1 part Black, shade the chimneys under the ledges with a no. 2 flat and under the roof trim on the front and side of the building with a no. 10 flat. With Fjord Blue, shade the top and left side of the roof with a no. 10 flat and the roof trim on the front and side of the building with a no. 2 flat. Paint the shingle lines on the roof with thinned Fjord Blue on a no. 10/0 liner. Paint the brick mortar lines on the chimneys and the building with thinned Mudstone on a no. 10/0 liner. When dry, transfer the main lines for the windows, doors, shutters and steps.

Base the stone ledges above the windows and doors on the front of the building with Mudstone and above the windows on the side of the building with a mixture of 1 part Mudstone + 1 part Fjord Blue. Base the window and door areas, including the ledges below the windows, with a mixture of 1 part Salem Green + 1 part Mudstone. Using Fjord Blue, base the shutters with a no. 1 flat and base the doors over the trim color with a no. 2 flat. Base the side of the steps with 1 part Slate Grey + 1 part Fjord Blue and the front of the steps with Slate Grey.

10 Finish the Bank

Paint the dentil moldings (the series of small projecting rectangular blocks) over the Fjord Blue shading in the center of the roof trim with Mudstone and a no. 10/0 flat. Float through the center of the trim with Fjord Blue again to shade the top of the notches. If your notches don't show, your shading wasn't dark enough before you applied the notches. If this area is too tiny for you, simply eliminate the center float and put the notches at the very top of the roof trim.

Highlight the top of a few of the shingles with Eggshell. Shade the window and door trim areas with Fjord Blue. Shade the top of the ledges above the doors and windows with

Shade and base the main areas of the bank, using a brush that fits the area you're painting. This enables you to paint the area in one stroke, resulting in a neater painting.

Complete the details.

Fjord Blue. Base the inside area of all windows with Black. Paint the pane lines in the windows with a mixture of 1 part Salem Green + 1 part Mudstone. Shade the right section of the steps with Black. Shade the bottom of each step on the Slate Grey area with Fjord Blue. Shade the left side of the shutters, the top and both sides of the door and the top and left side of each panel on the door and shutters with a mixture of 1 part Fjord Blue + 1 part Black. Outline the right and bottom of each panel on the shutters, and paint the louver lines in these panels with a thinned mix of 1 part Fjord Blue + 1 part Black. Dot the doorknobs with Black. Paint a thin Black line to the right of each left shutter. Shade under the windows with a mix of 1 part Black + 1 part Black Plum.

Using a no. 2 round, base the rocks

on the front of the foundation with Buttermilk and the rocks on the right side of the foundation with Eggshell. All remaining shading on this building is done with a no. 2 flat. Shade the bottom of each rock with Fjord Blue. Base the railings and the sign with Fjord Blue. Shade the sign and the railing with 1 part Fjord Blue + 1 part Black. Highlight the shutters, door, railing and sign with French Grey/Blue. Paint the lettering on the sign with thinned Antique Gold. Shade the lettering with thinned Light Cinnamon, using a no. 10/0 liner. Highlight the lettering with thinned Buttermilk, again using a liner. Outline the sign with Mudstone. Paint the bracket for the sign with thinned Black and a no. 10/0 liner. Highlight the bracket with thinned French Grey/Blue on a no. 10/0 liner.

11 Begin to Detail the Book Shoppe

Shade the front of the chimney above and below the ledge and the front of the building with Dark Chocolate. Shade the right side of the chimney and building with a mixture of 1 part Dark Chocolate + 1 part Black. Use a no. 4 flat for the chimney shading and a no. 10 flat for the main area of the building. Shade the roof with Black. Shade under the gable roofs and at the top of the main roof trim with Fjord Blue. Base the windows in the gables and the little opening at the top front of the chimney with Black. Paint all the brick mortar lines on the chimney and building with thinned Mudstone on a no. 10/0 liner. Base window and door areas on the front of the building with Buttermilk. Base the window areas on the side of the building with Eggshell. Base the shutters with Black.

Shade and base the main details of the book shoppe.

12 Finish the Book Shoppe

Use Black to base the inside area of all the windows and doors. Shade all the window and door trim areas with Fjord Blue. Add all highlights and shading in this step using a no. 2 flat. Paint the pane lines in the windows on the front of the building with thinned Buttermilk and a liner, and the pane lines in the windows on the right side of the building with thinned Eggshell. All liner work is done with a no. 10/0 liner and thinned paint. Base the sign and bracket with Black. Highlight the left side of the shutters, door and sign with French Grey/Blue. Highlight the sign bracket with thinned French Grey/Blue and a liner. Highlight the top of the gable roofs with French Grey/Blue. Paint the lettering on the sign following the directions for the signs on the other buildings. Paint the brass plaque on the door and the doorknobs with Antique Gold. Shade the bottom of the plaques and doorknobs with Light Cinnamon, and highlight the top with Buttermilk.

Complete the details.

13 Begin to Detail the House

Shade under the roof trim and next to the trim on the edges of the building with a mixture of 1 part Salem Green + 1 part Black on a no. 10 flat. Thin this mix to paint the lap siding lines. Shade the roof with Black and a no. 10 flat. Transfer the pattern for the windows, shutters, curtains, doorway and steps. Use a no. 2 round to paint the curtains and porch columns, and the appropriate-width flat brush for all remaining areas. Remember, one stroke looks better than using a brush that's too little, which will leave more ridges in your painting. Base the curtains with Mudstone and the area below the curtains with Black. Base the entire doorway, including the columns, and the shutters with Buttermilk. Base the door and steps with Mudstone and the windows above and to the sides of the door with Black.

Shade and base the main details of the house.

14 Finish the House

Shade the roof trim, curtains, door, all the Buttermilk areas around the door and the steps with Fjord Blue. All the remaining shading is done with a no. 2 flat. Base the window on the door with Black. Paint the pane lines in all the windows with thinned Buttermilk. Use a no. 10/0 liner for all the linework on the pane lines, shingles and other details. Outline the window on the door with Buttermilk. Outline the top of the porch roof and paint the shingle lines on the roof with thinned Black on a no. 10/0 liner. Dot the doorknob with Black. Paint two very thin Fjord Blue horizontal stripes on the ledge above the columns. Shade the left side of every shutter and the top and left side of each panel on the shutters with Slate Grey. Outline the right and bottom side of each panel on the shutters with thinned Slate Grey. Add a very tiny dot of Buttermilk in the center of the doorknob.

Complete the details.

15 Begin to Detail the Antique Shoppe

Shade under the roof and at the top of the first level of the shoppe with Dark Chocolate on a no. 10 flat. Paint the lap siding lines with thinned Dark Chocolate and a no. 10/0 liner. Shade the top and both ends of the roof with a mixture of 2 parts Light Cinnamon + 1 part Black on a no. 10 flat. Thin this mix and paint the shingle lines on the roof with a no. 10/0 liner. Highlight the top of a few shingles with Antique Gold on a no. 2 flat. Base all remaining areas with the appropriate-width flat brush. Shade the chimney with a mixture of 1 part Rookwood Red + 1 part Black. Transfer the pattern for the trim under the roof and on the edges of the building, the sign, window areas, door and brackets under the upper level. Base with Eggshell.

16 Finish the Antique Shoppe

Shade all the Eggshell areas with Fjord Blue on a no. 2 flat. Shade under the windows and the brackets with Dark Chocolate. Using Salem Green, base the door with a no. 6 flat and the inside area of the sign with a no. 2 flat. Base the inside area of all windows with Black on a no. 2 flat. Paint the pane lines in all windows with thinned Eggshell and a no. 10/0 liner. Using a mixture of 1 part Salem Green + 1 part Black, shade the door with a no. 6 flat and the sign with a no. 4 flat. Also use this mix to shade the top and left side of each door panel. Complete the remaining details using a no. 10/0 liner brush. Thin the mix and outline the right and bottom of the panels and paint the louver lines inside the panels. Paint the lettering on the sign and the door handle with Antique Gold. Shade the lettering and handle with thinned Light Cinnamon, and highlight with thinned Buttermilk. Shade to the right of the door handle with a mixture of 1 part Salem Green + 1 part Black. Paint the mortar lines on the chimney with thinned Mudstone.

Shade and base the main details of the antique shoppe.

Complete the details.

17 Paint the Clouds, Grass and Sidewalk

Paint one cloud at a time. If you stipple several clouds at once, you won't be able to come back and mop because the first clouds you stippled will already be dry. Use a ¾-inch (1.9cm) flat to dampen an area quite a bit larger than your cloud will actually be with a little water (no puddles). Quickly stipple the cloud formation with Buttermilk and an old, fuzzy no. 6 or no. 10 flat. Before the cloud dries, gently mop in all directions to soften the cloud.

Heavily stipple the grass between the buildings with Dark Forest Green on an old, fuzzy flat brush. Stipple lightly with Wedgwood Green, allowing the Dark Forest Green to show through. Base the sidewalk with Mudstone, and use a no. 16 flat to shade the top of the sidewalk with Fjord Blue (completed sidewalk shown on page 45). Stipple some grass down onto the shading with Dark Forest Green and Wedgwood Green.

Wet, stipple and mop the clouds with Buttermilk. Stipple the grass with Dark Forest Green.

If your clouds won't soften, you didn't mop quickly enough and the paint dried. If your clouds disappear when you mop, you're either using too much water or mopping too hard. Stipple the grass again with Wedgwood Green.

18 Paint the Trees and Fence

Heavily stipple the evergreen trees with Black on an old, fuzzy no. 2 flat. Base the trunks on the other trees with a mixture of 2 parts Dark Chocolate + 1 part Black, using a no. 10/0 liner. Thin this mix to paint the branches, again using a liner brush. Heavily stipple the tree foliage with Dark Forest Green.

Begin to separate the individual evergreen trees by lightly stippling the trees in front with Salem Green. Again using Salem Green, stipple the center (back) tree more heavily at the top and very lightly as it reaches the front trees. Form clumps of foliage on the other trees by stippling more heavily at the top of each clump with Mistletoe.

To add more dimension to the evergreens, stipple once again, very lightly, with a mixture of 2 parts Salem Green + 1 part Eggshell. Highlight the foliage on the other trees with just a little Bright Green at the top of each clump. Base the vertical slats on the fence

with Buttermilk on a no. 0 flat. Base the horizontal fence slats just as you did the vertical slats. Shade the left end of each horizontal slat on the fence with Fjord Blue and a no. 2 flat.

Stipple the trees with the darkest value. Always use a dry stipple brush. If you wet your brush, you won't get that crisp, fuzzy look.

Create depth by stippling with a lighter value, separating the individual trees.

Stipple with the lightest value. All three values on both types of trees should show through.

19 **Add the Bushes and Flowers**
Stipple the bushes in front of all the buildings with a fuzzy no. 2 flat, using a mixture of 1 part Dark Forest Green + 1 part Black. Stipple lightly with Dark Forest Green, and once again with Mistletoe. The Mistletoe should be heavier at the top of the bushes and lighter as you work your way down. Double-load an old, fuzzy no. 0 flat by dipping one corner of the brush into Rookwood Red and the other corner into Buttermilk. Tap the brush on the palette in the same place until the two colors have blended slightly in the center of the brush, then gently tap in the individual flowers.

Stipple the bushes with a mix of Dark Forest Green and Black, then again with Dark Forest Green.

Stipple lightly with Mistletoe, and tap in the double-loaded roses.

20 Paint the Streetlamps

Paint the glass areas of the lanterns with a transparent wash of Buttermilk and a no. 2 flat. Paint the remainder of the lamps with Black using a no. 10/0 liner. To highlight the lampposts, dampen with a little water and paint a line of thinned French Grey/Blue up the center of the post, then quickly mop to soften. Highlight the other Black sections with a liner and tiny dashes of French Grey/Blue.

21 Paint the Flag

Base the entire flag on the house with Buttermilk on a no. 10 flat. Base the blue area of the flag with Fjord Blue on a no. 6 flat. Paint the flagpole with Black on a liner brush. Base the stripes with Rookwood Red, using a no. 10/0 liner. Shade the left and right sides of the striped section with Fjord Blue on a no. 4 flat. Shade the blue area next to the pole with Black, and highlight the top with French Grey/Blue on a no. 4 flat. To create the stars, paint tiny Xs with thinned Buttermilk. Highlight the pole with thinned French Grey/Blue on a no. 10/0 liner.

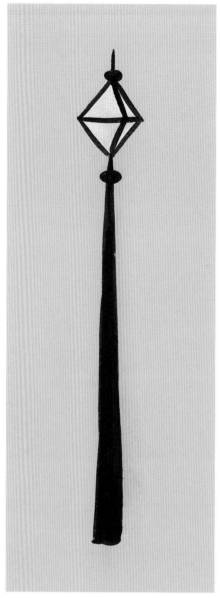

Base the lamps with Black and a wash of Buttermilk.

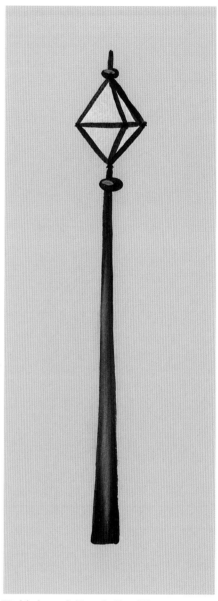

Highlight with French Grey/Blue.

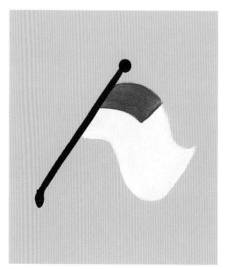

Base the flag.

Complete the details.

22 Finish the Bowl

Base the center of the bowl with Rookwood Red. Remove all graphite lines on the buildings with a Magic Rub eraser. Spray the bowl lightly two to three times with Krylon Matte Finish spray. Mix Burnt Umber oil paint and odorless turpentine to create an antiquing glaze. The antiquing should be dark but easy to spread. Apply with a 1-inch (2.5cm) sponge brush to the center of the bowl. Lay a piece of bubble wrap over the antiquing, and press evenly all over—don't move the bubble wrap, and don't pop any bubbles in the packing or you will leave blank spots in your faux finish. Carefully remove the bubble wrap, and, with a paper towel wrapped around your finger, gently blend any antiquing that squeezed onto the sidewalk. Allow to dry thoroughly. This will take twenty-four hours to dry completely, so if you're not happy with the effect, you can reapply the antiquing glaze and try again. If your design seems to bleed and won't stay put, you're using too much turpentine in the mix. Base the outside of the bowl with Salem Green. When dry, apply several coats of waterbase varnish.

Project 4
KITCHEN SET

This wooden flour sifter and matching salt and pepper shakers make a great set to display in your country kitchen. However, these designs could easily be painted around any object, or on any flat surface. If painted on a flat surface, be sure to take the part of the pond that appears in the lower left corner and move this to the right end of the picture, lining it up with the pattern. (When painting this on the salt and pepper shakers, the two sides of the pond join when the pattern is wrapped around the surfaces.)

MATERIALS

DecoArt Americana Acrylic Paints

Buttermilk DA3	Slate Grey DA68	Yellow Ochre DA8	Primary Yellow DA201	Raw Sienna DA93	Hauser Light Green DA131
Hauser Medium Green DA132	Mistletoe DA53	Bright Green DA54	Deep Teal DA116	True Red DA129	Country Red DA18
Napa Red DA165	Rookwood Red DA97	Medium Flesh DA102	Light Cinnamon DA114	Dark Chocolate DA65	

Delta Ceramcoat Acrylic Paints

White 02505	Mudstone 02488	Black 02506	Dark Forest Green 02096	Ocean Mist Blue 02529	Fjord Blue 02104
Burnt Sienna 02030	Santa Fe Rose 02496				

Materials List continued on page 50

❧ CHARMING VILLAGE SCENES YOU CAN PAINT ❧

© C. HolmAN 1998

This pattern for the flour sifter may be
hand-traced or photocopied for personal use
only. Reattach right and left halves of pattern, and enlarge at 133 percent to bring up
to full size.

© C. HolmAN 1998

This pattern for the salt and pepper shakers
may be hand-traced or photocopied for personal use only. Reattach right and left
sides; pattern appears at full size.

Loew Cornell Brushes
- Series 7300 nos. 10/0, 0, 1, 2, 4, 6, 10 and 16 flat shaders
- Series 7550 ¾-inch (1.9cm) wash brush
- Series 275 ¾-inch (1.9cm) mop brush
- Series 7000 no. 2 round
- Series 7350 no. 10/0 liner (short)
- Jackie Shaw no. 10/0 liner
- Old, fuzzy flats for stippling

Other Supplies
- 1-inch (2.5cm) sponge brush
- Stain of your choice
- Tracing paper
- White and gray graphite paper
- Scotch Magic Transparent Tape
- Viva paper towels
- J.W. etc. Right-Step matte waterbase varnish
- Magic Rub eraser
- Transparent grid ruler
- Designs From the Heart wood sealer
- 400-grit black wet/dry sandpaper

Surface
The wooden salt and pepper shakers (4⅜″ × 2⅝″ [11cm × 14cm]) and flour sifter (6¾″ × 5⅞″ [17cm × 15cm]) are available from:
Steph's Folk Art Studio
2435 Old Philadelphia Pike
Smoketown, PA 17576
(717) 299-4973

1 Prepare the Surface and Basecoat
Using a 1-inch (2.5cm) sponge brush, apply the wood sealer according to the directions on the bottle. When dry, sand with 400-grit black wet/dry sandpaper. Trace your pattern onto tracing paper, and tape to the surface. With gray graphite under your tracing, transfer only the line that separates the ground from the sky area; do this for the flour sifter and the salt and pepper shakers. Base the sky areas with Ocean Mist Blue and the ground with Dark Forest Green using a ¾-inch (1.9cm) wash brush.

Base the sky with Ocean Mist Blue and the ground with Dark Forest Green.

2 Stipple the Clouds and Grass
Dampen the sky using a ¾-inch (1.9cm) wash brush and clean water. Stipple a cloud with Buttermilk on an old, fuzzy no. 10 flat, and quickly, but gently, mop to soften. Stipple and mop only one cloud at a time, allowing each to dry before doing the next. Repeat these same steps, stippling White at the top of each cloud to highlight.

Stipple the grass with Hauser Medium Green and a fuzzy no. 10 flat, stippling more heavily at the top of the ground area and lighter as you work your way down. Repeat with Hauser Light Green, only bringing this color about two-thirds of the way down.

Stipple the clouds with Buttermilk, then White. Stipple the grass with Hauser Medium Green and repeat with Hauser Light Green.

3 Begin to Paint the House

Transfer only the main lines for the house on the flour sifter. Base the main area of the house with Mudstone, and the roof sections with Deep Teal. Base the fish scale shingle section in the upper peak of the house with Hauser Medium Green. Base the roof trim, porch posts on the front of the house and railing with Buttermilk on a no. 2 round. Paint the foundation and the underside of the small back porch roof with a mixture of 1 part Mudstone + 1 part Fjord Blue.

Shade below the Buttermilk roof trim on the Mudstone areas of the house and between the front and back sections of the house with the Mudstone + Fjord Blue mix. Thin this mix and paint the lap siding lines on this area of the house using a no. 10/0 liner. Shade the Buttermilk areas with Slate Grey using a no. 2 flat. Apply tape to the roof of the house to keep it clean, and begin heavily stippling the tree foliage behind the house with a mixture of 1 part Dark Forest Green + 1 part Black. Stipple lightly with Mistletoe, keeping the stippling heavier at the top of the tree foliage. Repeat with Bright Green.

4 Complete the Details on the House

Shade the foundation with Fjord Blue. Shade the roof areas with a mixture of 1 part Deep Teal + 1 part Black. Use this mix to shade the fish scale shingle section and to paint the shingles, thinning the paint and using a no. 10/0 liner for the latter. Transfer the main lines for all the windows. Base the windows with Buttermilk, using a brush that fits the size of each window for a smoother basecoat.

Base the little roof section above the large double window with Deep Teal, and the trim above and below this roof with Buttermilk. Shade the top of each Buttermilk window with Slate Grey. Shade the roof above the window with a mixture of 1 part Deep Teal + 1 part Black. Base the inside area of all windows with a mixture of 1 part Slate Grey + 1 part Black. Shade the top and left side of the grey windows with Black.

The following details are shown completed on page 61. Using a no. 10/0 liner and thinned Buttermilk, paint the pane lines in the windows and the trim on the edges of the house. Paint the remaining porch posts and railings with Buttermilk. Shade the porch posts and railings with Slate Grey, and strengthen some of these areas with Fjord Blue. Paint the brick mortar lines on the foundation of the house with thinned Mudstone and a no. 10/0 liner. Paint a thin Black line along the edge of all the roof areas.

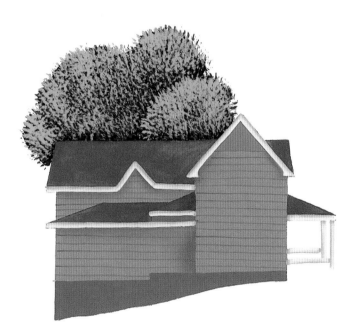

Base the house and protect the roof with tape before stippling the tree foliage behind the house, or stipple the tree first and then base the house. Hold the liner brush perpendicular to the surface when painting the siding lines.

Complete the house.

5 Begin to Paint the Barn

Using a ¾-inch (1.9cm) wash brush, base the left side of the barn on the flour sifter with Napa Red and the front of the barn with a mixture of 4 parts Napa Red + 1 part Black. Base the roof of the barn with Country Red and the roof overhang with a mixture of 4 parts Country Red + 1 part Black, using a no. 4 or no. 6 flat.

6 Complete the Main Areas of the Barn

Base the door opening with Black. Tape off the roof and stipple the tree foliage behind the barn following the directions in step three. Shade the side of the barn with a mixture of 2 parts Napa Red + 1 part Black. Thin this mix and paint the siding lines on the side using a no. 10/0 liner. Shade the front of the barn with Black, and paint the siding lines with thinned Black. Base the inside area of the window on the side of the barn with Black. Paint the shutters with Fjord Blue, and the sign below the window with Buttermilk using a no. 6 flat. Shade the main area of the roof with a mixture of 2 parts Country Red + 1 part Black. Thin this mix and paint the lines on the roof with a no. 10/0 liner. Add more Black to the mix to shade the roof overhang on the front of the barn. Outline the sign below the window with thinned Black. Shade the top and both ends of the Buttermilk sign with Fjord Blue. Paint the lettering with Black. Float above and below the horizontal slats on the shutters with a mixture of 1 part Fjord Blue + 1 part Black, then paint a thin line below these horizontal slats with this same mix. Paint the vertical lines on the shutters with thinned Black and a liner.

The following details are shown completed on page 60. Highlight the top of the horizontal slats on the shutters with a mixture of 1 part Fjord Blue + 1 part Buttermilk. Dampen the side of the barn with clear water, then highlight between some of the siding lines with a liner and a thin streak of Country Red. Mop in a vertical direction. Highlight between some of the lines on the roof in the same manner, using True Red. Highlight the floor of the barn with a no. 10 flat and Fjord Blue. Base the flag with Black, and highlight the top of the flag with Fjord Blue. Paint the sunflowers on the flag and over the door as instructed in step seven. Paint the flagpole with Light Cinnamon, and shade with a mixture of 1 part Light Cinnamon + 1 part Black. Highlight the pole by dampening with a little water, then streaking a couple of dashes of thinned Yellow Ochre on the pole. Mop to soften. Base the road with Mudstone, and shade with Fjord Blue. Stipple the grass over the edges of the road with Hauser Medium Green and again with Hauser Light Green.

Base the barn.

Complete the main details.

7 Paint the Details Inside the Window

Paint the bag inside the barn window with Mudstone, and the hay bale with Raw Sienna. Shade the bag and the hay bale with Light Cinnamon. Repeat with Dark Chocolate. Highlight the bag with Buttermilk, and paint the string at the neck of the bag with thinned Dark Chocolate. Flick the lines on the hay bale with thinned Yellow Ochre and a liner, and then shade once again with Dark Chocolate. Base the sunflower centers with Light Cinnamon. Paint the stems with Dark Forest Green and a liner. Highlight the flower centers with Yellow Ochre, and shade with a mixture of 1 part Light Cinnamon + 1 part Black. To paint the petals on the sunflowers, load a short no. 10/0 liner with thinned Primary Yellow, then dip the tip of the brush into thick paint so you have a tiny glob of paint on the end of the brush. Now, starting at the flower center, flick the petals on all the way around the center. The petals on the back of the flower should be shorter than the petals on the front of the flower.

The sunflower leaves are double-loaded S-strokes, done by dipping one corner of a no. 2 flat into Dark Forest Green and the other corner into Mistletoe. Blend the colors in the center of your brush by stroking the brush on your palette in one direction, then flipping the brush over to blend the other side of the brush in the same strip on your palette (keeping the Dark Forest Green side of the brush in the Dark Forest Green area of the palette). Blend back and forth in this manner in the same strip three or four times, until the two colors are blended in the center of the brush. The stroke is executed in a calligraphy style: Use the chisel edge of the brush at the beginning and end of the stroke.

Base and shade the bag, hay bale and sunflower centers.

Paint the sunflower petals and leaves, and detail the bag and hay bale.

8 Paint the Shelves

Base the shelves on the side of the barn with a no. 2 round and Mudstone. Base the flowerpots on the shelves with Santa Fe Rose and the watering cans with Slate Grey, using a no. 2 round or a small flat.

Shade the flowerpots with Rookwood Red and the watering cans with Fjord Blue, using a no. 2 or no. 4 flat.

Dampen the watering cans with a little water, highlight with Buttermilk on a liner and mop to soften. Float the bottom edge of the shelves with Fjord Blue on a no. 2 flat, then shade under the shelves with a mixture of 1 part Napa Red + 1 part Black. Heavily stipple the flower foliage in the flowerpots with Dark Forest Green, and then lightly with Mistletoe. Paint the flowers with an old, fuzzy no. 0 flat, double-loaded with Rookwood Red and Buttermilk, as instructed in step nine.

Base the shelf, flowerpots and watering cans.

Shade the flowerpots and watering cans.

Complete the shelves.

9 Paint the Foliage Below the Barn

Heavily stipple the flower foliage at the bottom of the barn and house with a mixture of 1 part Dark Forest Green + 1 part Black, using an old, fuzzy no. 2 or no. 4 flat. Repeat lightly with Dark Forest Green, then with Mistletoe. The flowers are done with an old, fuzzy no. 2 flat, double-loaded with Napa Red on one corner of the brush and Buttermilk on the other. Tap the brush on the palette to blend the two colors in the center of the brush, and then tap the individual flowers on top of the flower foliage.

The sunflowers at the back of the barn and below the house are done in the same way as those in the barn window, but use a no. 4 flat for the leaves on the flowers by the barn.

Stipple the flower foliage with Dark Forest Green + Black.

Stipple the foliage again lightly with Dark Forest Green.

Repeat the stippling again lightly with Mistletoe, stippling more heavily at the top.

Add the flowers.

10 Paint the Clothesline

Base the clothesline poles with Slate Grey and a no. 2 round. Shade with Fjord Blue and a no. 4 flat. Paint the lines between the poles with thinned Fjord Blue and a no. 10/0 liner. Base the sheets, T-shirt and socks with Buttermilk. Base the towels and washcloths with a mixture of 1 part Buttermilk + 1 part Primary Yellow. Shade the Buttermilk sheets and clothes with Slate Grey on a no. 4 flat. Reinforce the shading on the fitted sheet with Fjord Blue. Paint the stripes on the sheets with a mixture of 1 part Deep Teal + 1 part White and a liner. Paint the stripes on the socks with Rookwood Red and a liner. Shade the towels and washcloths with Raw Sienna on a no. 4 flat. Also use Raw Sienna to paint the clothespins with a liner and to base the laundry basket on the ground with a no. 2 flat. Shade the basket with Dark Chocolate and highlight with Primary Yellow, using a no. 2 flat for both. Shade inside the basket again with 1 part Dark Chocolate + 1 part Black. Paint the handles with thinned Black on a liner. Highlight the handles with thinned Slate Grey on a liner. Flick some grass up around the bottom of the basket with thinned Hauser Light Green and a liner.

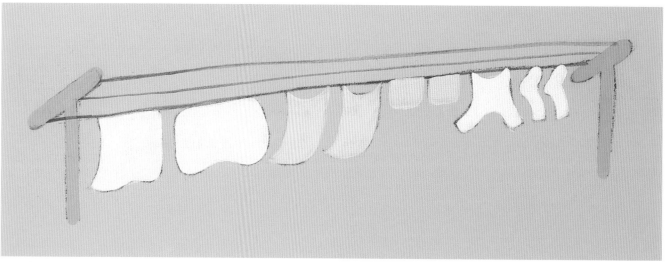

Base the laundry and clothesline.

Complete the laundry, clothesline and basket.

11 Paint the Birdhouse and Girl

Use small flats or a no. 2 round to base all areas in this step. Base the birdhouse and post with Buttermilk and the roof with Black. Shade the birdhouse and post with Fjord Blue on a no. 4 or no. 6 flat. Outline the top center roof peak, and base the hole with Black. Stipple the foliage and flowers around the base of the birdhouse as instructed in step nine. Base the girl's face, arms and legs with Medium Flesh, her shirt with Rookwood Red, her shorts with Fjord Blue, her hair with Raw Sienna and her shoes with Buttermilk. Using a no. 2 or no. 4 flat, shade her face, arms and legs with Burnt Sienna. Shade her shirt with 1 part Rookwood Red + 1 part Black. Shade her shorts with 1 part Fjord Blue + 1 part Black. Shade her shoes with Fjord Blue and her hair with Dark Chocolate. Highlight her hair with Primary Yellow.

Base the birdhouse and the girl.

Shade the birdhouse and girl. Stipple the flowers at the base of the post.

12 Paint the Distant House, Man and Dog

Base the left side of the house with a mixture of 1 part Buttermilk + 1 part Slate Grey and the front end of the house with Slate Grey. Base the roofs with Black. Base the door and the left side of the chimney with Rookwood Red, and the right side with a mixture of 3 parts Rookwood Red + 1 part Black. Shade under the roofs on the house and between the two sections with Fjord Blue. Base the windows and the porch roof with Black. Shade under the porch roof with Fjord Blue. Shade the chimney and door with a darker value of the Rookwood Red + Black mix (add more Black). Paint the detailed linework on the house with thinned Buttermilk. Stipple the bushes below the house with a mixture of 1 part Dark Forest Green + 1 part Black, then with Dark Forest Green and again with Mistletoe. Base the man's neck, arms and legs with Medium Flesh. Base his hat and shorts with Fjord Blue and his shirt and shoes with Buttermilk. Base the dog with Raw Sienna. Use a no. 2 flat to shade the man and dog. Shade his flesh areas with Burnt Sienna, his shorts and hat with Black and his shirt and shoes with Fjord Blue. Base the hair below his hat with Dark Chocolate. Shade the dog with Dark Chocolate. Highlight the dog with Primary Yellow. Flick a few hairs on the tail with thinned Primary Yellow and a liner. Paint the dog collar Black. Base the tree trunks with Dark Chocolate, and shade with a mixture of 1 part Dark Chocolate + 1 part Black on the left side of the trunk. Stipple the foliage heavily with Dark Forest Green, then lightly with Mistletoe, followed by Bright Green. Stipple the flowers and foliage at the base of the tree.

Base the house in the distance, the man and dog.

Add shading and detail to the house. Stipple the bushes. Shade the man and dog.

13 Paint the Sign

Base the center of the sign with Buttermilk. Paint the posts with Dark Chocolate. Outline the top and bottom of the sign and base the arrow with Black. Shade the top and both ends of the Buttermilk area with Fjord Blue. Shade the left side of the posts with a mixture of 1 part Dark Chocolate + 1 part Black. Highlight the right side of the posts with Raw Sienna. Highlight the arrow with Fjord Blue. Paint the lettering with thinned Black. Stipple the flowers at the base of the posts as in previous steps.

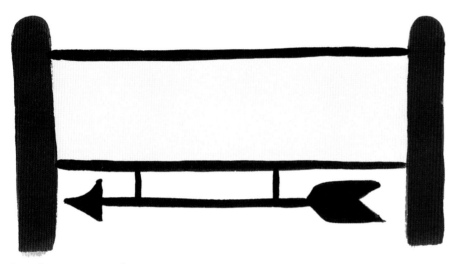

Base the sign, posts and arrow.

Shade and highlight the sign and posts. Stipple the flowers below the posts. When painting lettering, count the letters and paint the middle letter first so you know it will be centered.

14 Paint the Scarecrow

Base the scarecrow's face with Mudstone, the hat with Yellow Ochre, the shirt with Buttermilk, the pants with Fjord Blue and the scarf with Rookwood Red. Paint the crow's body with Black and the beak and feet with Primary Yellow. Shade the scarecrow's face with Fjord Blue. Paint the stripes on the shirt with thinned Rookwood Red and a liner. Shade the shirt with Fjord Blue. Shade the scarf with a mixture of 1 part Rookwood Red + 1 part Black, and highlight with True Red. Shade the pants with a mixture of 1 part Fjord Blue + 1 part Black, and highlight with Ocean Mist Blue. Shade the hat with Raw Sienna, then again with Light Cinnamon. Also shade the beak on the crow with Light Cinnamon. Paint the straw on the hands, neck and under the hat with Raw Sienna and repeat with Yellow Ochre.

Shade the straw with Light Cinnamon. Highlight the crow with Fjord Blue. Paint the daisy stems below the scarecrow with a thinned mixture of 1 part Dark Forest Green + 1 part Black

using a liner. Paint the centers of the flowers Primary Yellow and the petals Buttermilk. Use a liner dipped into thick paint and simply tap them in.

Base the scarecrow.

Add the details. The flower stems should be applied heavily enough that the bottom of the scarecrow pants are obscured.

Add the remaining detail and your own special touches. Paint the band and sunflowers at the bottom of the sifter.

15 Finish the Flour Sifter

Measure a ½" (1cm) band around the bottom of the flour sifter. Apply tape above this line, pressing the tape firmly along the lower edge. Base this band, the handle, the knob on the crank and the top and bottom edges of the sifter with Black. Base the sunflower centers with Light Cinnamon. Highlight the centers with Yellow Ochre, and shade with a mixture of 1 part Light Cinnamon + 1 part Black. Paint the petals with Primary Yellow and a liner, starting at the center and stroking away. Paint the comma strokes between the flowers on the band and the vine on the handle with Hauser Medium Green. Paint the leaves on the band and the handle with a no. 6 flat double-loaded with Dark Forest Green and Mistletoe. Shade above the band on the sifter with Dark Chocolate, using a no. 16 flat. You could also paint a sunflower on the knob on the end of the crank as I did. Stain the inside of the sifter. Finish the wooden areas of the sifter with Right-Step varnish.

Base the handle with Black. Paint the vine with thinned paint and a liner. Paint the leaves with a double-loaded no. 6 flat, using S-strokes.

16 Base the Salt and Pepper Shakers

Base the tree trunks with Dark Chocolate. Shade the left side of the trunks with Black. Stipple the foliage heavily with Dark Forest Green. Repeat lightly with Mistletoe, and again with Bright Green. Stipple the evergreen trees heavily with Black. Stipple lightly with Deep Teal, leaving a shadow between the two in the distance. On the distant evergreens only, stipple lightly with a mixture of 4 parts Deep Teal + 1 part Buttermilk.

Base the main area of the house with Mudstone, the roof with Black and the chimneys with Rookwood Red. Base the barn with Rookwood Red, the silo with Mudstone, the silo roof with Slate Grey and the roof trim with Buttermilk. Base the barn in the lower foreground with Napa Red, the right side of the cupola with Napa Red, the left side of the cupola with a mixture of 4 parts Napa Red + 1 part Black, the roof with Black, the right side of the cupola roof with Slate Grey, the left side with a mixture of 4 parts Slate Grey + 1 part Black and the weather vane with thinned Black. Base the wagon with Deep Teal. Base the pond with Ocean Mist Blue.

17 Finish the Salt and Pepper Shakers

Shade below the roofs with Fjord Blue. Shade the chimneys with a mixture of 1 part Rookwood Red + 1 part Black. Base the windows with a no. 6 flat and Black. Base the door with a no. 4 flat and Deep Teal. Shade the top and left side of the door with a mixture of 1 part Deep Teal + 1 part Black. Highlight the right side of the door with a mixture of 1 part Deep Teal + 1 part Buttermilk. Paint the window on the door with a no. 2 flat and Black. Paint the door handle Black, and outline the top of the peak on the porch roof with thinned Black. Paint all remaining trim with Buttermilk, using a liner. Shade some of the Buttermilk areas with Fjord Blue.

Shade between the two hills with a mixture of 1 part Dark Forest Green + 1 part Black. Shade the edges of the pond with Fjord Blue. Highlight the center of the pond with Buttermilk. Dampen the pond with a little water, paint the tree trunk reflection with thinned Dark Chocolate and quickly mop horizontally to blur. Allow to dry between each step. Dampen again and stipple the foliage reflection with Dark Forest Green and quickly mop. Repeat

the stippling again with Mistletoe and then with Bright Green, dampening and mopping between each color application. Dampen again and stipple the evergreen reflections with an old, fuzzy no. 2 flat and Black, then mop. Repeat with Deep Teal. Dampen the water below the barn, streak a little red in the water below the barn and quickly mop. Add the shine lines with thinned Buttermilk and a no. 10/0 liner. Base the paths with Mudstone, and shade with Dark Chocolate. Stipple the grass onto the edges of the paths with Hauser Medium Green and then with Hauser Light Green. Also, stipple below the pond and the shading between the two hills with these colors.

Shade below the roof and inside the door of the barn with a mixture of 1 part Rookwood Red + 1 part Black. Thin this mix to paint the siding lines. Paint the trim around the door with thinned Buttermilk. Paint a Black line to divide the two doors in the center. Outline along the top edge of the Buttermilk roof trim with Black. Shade the silo and silo roof with Fjord Blue, and highlight with Buttermilk. Paint the fence with a liner and thinned Dark Chocolate.

Shade the wagon with a mixture of

1 part Deep Teal + 1 part Black. Thin this mix to paint the wood grain on the wagon, using a liner. Highlight the side of the wagon with a mixture of 1 part Deep Teal + 1 part Buttermilk. Paint the wheels and the wagon tongue with thinned Black and a liner, and highlight with thinned Ocean Mist Blue. Paint the hay in the wagon with a liner and Raw Sienna, Primary Yellow and then Yellow Ochre. Flick a few blades of grass around the wagon wheels with thinned Hauser Light Green.

Shade the Napa Red areas of the barn in the foreground with a mixture of 1 part Napa Red + 1 part Black. Shade the left side of the cupola with a darker value (more Black) of the same mix. Highlight the roof with Fjord Blue. Base the window with Black. Paint the trim along the roof edges and around the window with thinned Buttermilk and a liner. Highlight the weather vane with thinned Ocean Mist Blue.

Base the top and bottom of the salt and pepper shakers with Black. Finish the shakers with several coats of Right-Step varnish. To clean the salt and pepper shakers and flour sifter, wipe with a damp cloth. Do not submerse in water.

Project 5
AUTUMN TABLE RUNNER

Canvas is such a great, inexpensive item to paint on. It comes precut in various shapes and sizes, or you can simply buy a large roll of it and cut any size you like. The great thing about this particular canvas is that it comes pre-primed on one side. This particular piece was cut from a 2′ × 3′ (61cm × 91cm) floorcloth. You can cut two runners from a floorcloth this size. If you would like to make this table runner more versatile, simply prep the other side with gesso, applying two to three coats with a sponge roller, and paint a winter scene on the opposite side. If you prep and paint on both sides of both runners, you could paint four different seasons. Have fun with it!

MATERIALS

DecoArt Americana Acrylic Paints

Black Green DA157	Slate Grey DA68	Charcoal Grey DA88	Moon Yellow DA7	Raw Sienna DA93	Pumpkin DA13
Burnt Orange DA16	French Grey/ Blue DA98	Uniform Blue DA86	Shale Green DA152	Hauser Light Green DA131	Hauser Medium Green DA132
Medium Flesh DA102	Rookwood Red DA97				

DecoArt Americana

Emperor's Gold DA148

Delta Ceramcoat

Butter Cream 02523	Black 02506	Dark Forest Green 02096
Fjord Blue 02104	Burnt Sienna 02030	Dark Burnt Umber 02527

Materials List continued on page 66

This pattern may be hand-traced or photocopied for personal use only. Reattach left and right halves, and enlarge at 200 percent, then again at 115 percent to bring up to full size.

1 Prepare the Canvas and Paint the Ground

This canvas comes preprimed on one side. (The primed side is a brighter white and is generally rolled to the inside when you get it.) If you only plan to paint on one side of the canvas, there is no prep. If you want to paint on both sides, apply two to three coats of gesso to the back side of the canvas.

Using a sponge roller, base the entire primed side of the canvas with two to three coats of Uniform Blue. When dry, use a grid ruler to mark a 1″ (2.5cm) border all the way around the canvas with a pencil. Base this border with a ¾-inch (1.9cm) wash brush and Rookwood Red. Tape won't stick firmly enough to this canvas to be able to tape off the border before basing, so just be very careful and apply several thin coats instead of one or two heavy coats.

Transfer the lines for the top of the ground line, and the main lines only for the house. Base the ground area with Black Green. Stipple the entire ground area with Dark Forest Green. Transfer the lines that separate the hills. Shade between the hills with Black Green, and stipple the ground again with Hauser Medium Green, stippling more heavily at the top of the hills.

MATERIALS CONTINUED

Loew Cornell Brushes
- Series 7300 nos. 10/0, 0, 1, 2, 4, 6, 10 and 16 flat shaders
- Series 7550 ¾-inch (1.9cm) wash brush
- Series 275 ¾-inch (1.9cm) mop brush
- Series 7000 no. 2 round
- Series 7350 no. 10/0 liner (short)
- Jackie Shaw no. 10/0 liner
- Assorted sizes of old, fuzzy flats for stippling

Other Supplies
- Sponge roller
- Tracing paper
- White and gray graphite paper
- J.W. etc. Right-Step matte waterbase varnish
- Transparent grid ruler
- Magic Rub eraser
- Scotch Magic Transparent Tape
- Gesso (optional)

Surface
This 9½″ × 34″ (24cm × 86cm) canvas table runner is available from:
An Americana Collection
103 Lakeview Dr.
Excelsior Springs, MO 64024
(816) 630-5832

2 Base and Shade the House

Base the main area of the house with Shale Green on a ¾-inch (1.9cm) wash brush (use a no. 10 flat for the peak) and the roof areas with Black on a no. 10 flat. Float shading next to the roof trim and under the porch roof with a no. 10 flat and a mixture of 1 part Shale Green + 1 part Charcoal Grey. Also use this mix to float shading under the roof on the right wing of the house and on the left side of this section, using a no. 16 flat. Dampen the area before you float, and mop the float quickly but gently before it dries. Thin the previous mix to paint the lap siding lines, using a no. 10/0 liner. The siding is much easier to do before the windows and door are added.

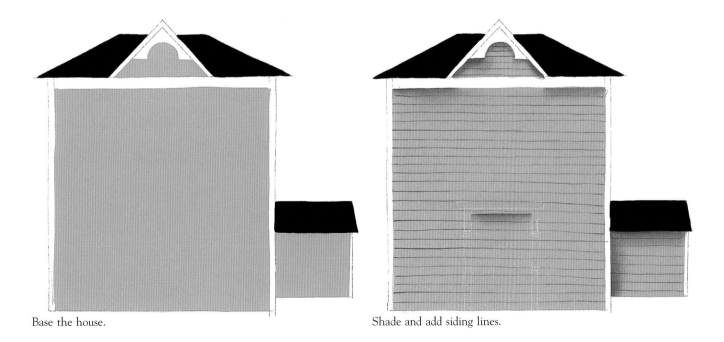

Base the house.   Shade and add siding lines.

3 Paint the Top Unlit Windows

Base the two unlit windows at the top with Butter Cream, using a no. 10 or no. 16 flat. Base the shutters with a no. 10 flat using a mixture of 1 part Shale Green + 1 part Charcoal Grey. Shade below the ledge at the top of the window and next to the shutters with a no. 6 flat and Fjord Blue. Base the inside area of the two unlit windows with Black, using a no. 6 flat. Basing in this order creates a much smoother finish, rather than trying to paint the Butter Cream around the Black. Paint the pane lines with thinned Butter Cream and a no. 10/0 liner (shown completed on pages 72–73).

4 Paint the Lower Lit Windows

Paint the lower lit windows in the same way as the unlit windows, leaving out the Black. Instead, shade the top and both sides of the curtains with Fjord Blue to separate them from the window trim of the same color. Base the area between the curtains with Moon Yellow. Float Burnt Sienna next to the curtain on the left side of the Moon Yellow area. Float Fjord Blue gathers on the curtains with a no. 2 flat. Paint the pane lines with thinned Butter Cream and a no. 10/0 liner.

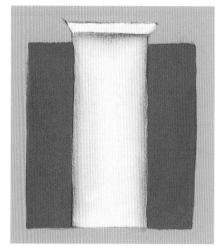
Base the unlit windows.

Fill in the windows.

Base the lit windows.

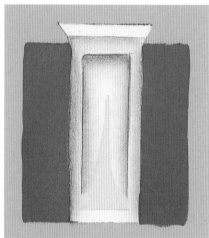
Base the area between the curtains.

Add shading and pane lines.

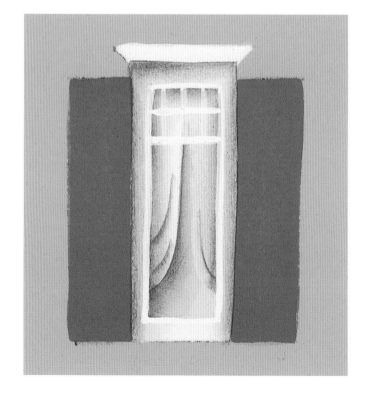

CHARMING VILLAGE SCENES YOU CAN PAINT

5 Paint the Upper Door

Base the upper door with Butter Cream. Shade with Fjord Blue. Using Moon Yellow, base the narrow window on the door with a no. 4 flat and the large window on the upper door with a no. 10 flat. Shade the top and left side of each yellow window with Burnt Sienna. Paint the trim on the door with a liner and thinned Butter Cream.

6 Paint the Porch, Lower Door and Remaining Details

Base the railing, porch roof, posts and door with Butter Cream. Shade with Fjord Blue. Base the door with Rookwood Red. Base the transom window with a no. 4 or no. 6 flat and Moon Yellow. Base the lower section of the door (over the red) with Slate Grey and a no. 10 flat. This is the main door area showing through the screen door. Base the window above the grey section with Butter Cream and a no. 10 flat. Base the area between the curtains on the lower window with Moon Yellow, using a no. 2 round. (This is easier than basing the window with yellow and then trying to paint the Butter Cream curtain over top.) Shade next to the curtain on the left side of the lower window and the top and left side of the transom window with Burnt Sienna. Shade the right, left and bottom of the grey door area with Fjord Blue. Shade the top and right side of the two left panels on the door and the top and left side of the two right panels with a no. 4 flat and Fjord Blue. Using Fjord Blue, shade the top and sides of the Butter Cream curtain area with a no. 4 flat and the gathers with a no. 2 flat. Paint the window and door trim with thinned Butter Cream and a liner, and dot the doorknob with straight Butter Cream.

Base the trim on the edges of the house, the roof trim and gingerbread in the upper peak with Butter Cream and a no. 10/0 liner. Shade all the Butter Cream areas with Fjord Blue. Base the porch floor with a mixture of 1 part

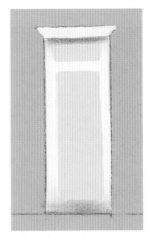

Base the upper door.

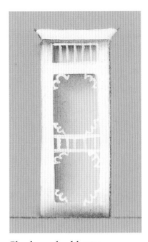

Fill in the windows.

Shade and add trim.

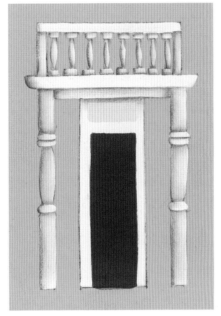

Paint the railing and posts, and base the door.

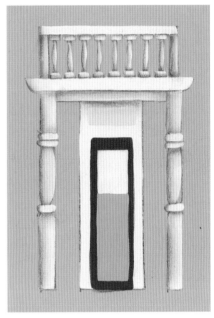

Base the inner sections of the door.

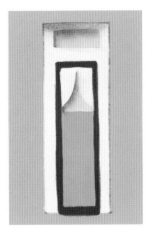

Fill in and shade the windows.

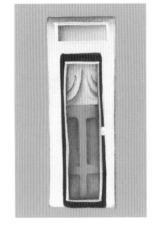

Shade the door panels and curtains, and add the trim and doorknob.

Shale Green + 1 part Charcoal Grey. Shade the porch floor with Charcoal Grey. Thin this color and paint the detail lines on the shutters and porch

floor with a no. 10/0 liner. Paint a thin line of Black along the top edge of the peak on the main roof, and outline along the top edge of the porch roof.

7 Paint the Foliage, Sidewalk and Fence

The following details are shown completed on pages 72–73. Heavily stipple the bushes below the house with Black Green. Stipple the bushes again, more heavily at the top, with Hauser Medium Green. Repeat the stippling once again with a mixture of 1 part Hauser Medium Green + 1 part Moon Yellow. Stipple the tops of the bushes directly below the windows with Moon Yellow.

Base the sidewalk with Slate Grey. Shade the sidewalk with Fjord Blue. Restipple the edges of the sidewalk with the grass colors: Dark Forest Green and Hauser Medium Green. Wet, float and mop the glow from the yellow windows with a ¾-inch (1.9cm) wash brush and Moon Yellow.

Base the fence with Butter Cream, and shade the posts with Slate Grey. Shade the railing where it attaches to the left side of each post with Fjord Blue.

8 Paint the Pumpkins

Base the pumpkins with Burnt Orange. Highlight the top of each pumpkin with Pumpkin. Shade the bottom of each pumpkin with a no. 10 flat and a mixture of 3 parts Rookwood Red + 1 part Black. Float the rib lines with the same mixture on a no. 2 flat. Float a little Moon Yellow on the tops of the pumpkins that are below the windows. Base the features on the jack-o'-lanterns with Moon Yellow and a liner. Shade inside the openings with Burnt Sienna on a no. 2 flat. Highlight inside the openings with a fleck of Butter Cream, using a liner. Outline the top of the mouth and to the left of the eyes and nose with a mixture of 3 parts Rookwood Red + 1 part Black. Outline along the lower edge of the eyes, nose and mouth with Pumpkin. Paint the stems with a liner and Black. Paint the leaves around the bases of the pumpkins with an old, fuzzy no. 2 flat double-loaded with Rookwood Red on one corner of the brush and Pumpkin

on the other. Tap the loaded brush up and down on the palette in the same spot to blend the colors in the center of the brush.

Base the pumpkins with Burnt Orange, and highlight the tops with Pumpkin.

Shade the bottom of the pumpkins, and float rib lines.

Paint the stems. Base the features on the jack-o'-lanterns, and shade the left side of the eyes and nose and the top of the mouth.

Outline outside the eyes, nose and mouth. Add a sparkle in the right side of the eyes with a fleck of Butter Cream, using a liner. Tap in a few leaves at the base of the pumpkins.

9 Paint the Distant Tree Foliage

Steps nine and ten are shown completed on pages 72–73. Heavily stipple the distant tree foliage (in the center of the runner behind the back hill) with Dark Forest Green. Stipple in a few red trees here and there throughout the foliage with Rookwood Red. Repeat on top of the Rookwood Red with Burnt Orange and then with Pumpkin at the top. Stipple the green trees with Hauser Medium Green, and repeat with Hauser Light Green at the tops. Stipple the yellow trees with Hauser Medium Green, then with 1 part Hauser Medium Green + 1 part Moon Yellow (brush mixed). Finish by stippling a touch of Moon Yellow at the top. Float the bottom of all the distant tree foliage with a no. 10 or no. 12 flat, using Black Green. Restipple the grass at the top of the hill with Hauser Medium Green. Outline along the inner edge of the Rookwood Red border with thinned Emperor's Gold.

10 Paint the Foreground Trees

Base the trees with Dark Burnt Umber. Shade the left side of the trunk on the large tree on the far right with Black. Double-load a fuzzy no. 2 flat with Rookwood Red on one corner and Pumpkin on the other, and stipple the leaves on the trees by the house and on the ground. Use a no. 4 or no. 6 fuzzy flat for the leaves on the far right tree and on the ground below the tree.

11 Base the Children

Base the faces, necks and hands on all the children with Medium Flesh, using nos. 10/0, 0 and 1 flat shaders. Base the jeans on the child in the swing with French Grey/Blue, and all the other jeans with Uniform Blue. Paint the hat on the boy in the swing with Rookwood Red. Base the girl's sweatshirt with Moon Yellow. Base the girl's hair and the sweatshirt on the boy in the swing with Raw Sienna. Using Black, base the tire swing, the sweatshirt on the boy lying down, the

Base the children, using the flat brush that best fills the area you are painting using the fewest amount of strokes. You can also flatten a no. 2 round for some of the smaller areas.

Shade, highlight and add final details to the children.

shoes on the boy in the swing and the bag of leaves. Base the sweatshirt on the boy raking the leaves with Slate Grey. Paint the hair on all the boys with Dark Burnt Umber. Paint the rake handle with Raw Sienna and the prongs with thinned Black. Base the remaining shoes with Butter Cream.

12 Add Detail to the Children
Shade and highlight the children's clothing with a no. 4 or no. 6 flat. Shade all the Uniform Blue jeans with Black. Shade the French Grey/Blue jeans with Uniform Blue. Highlight the Uniform Blue jeans with French Grey/Blue and the jeans on the boy in the swing with a mixture of 1 part French Grey/Blue + 2 parts Butter Cream. Shade the grey sweatshirt and the Butter Cream tennis shoes with Fjord Blue. Highlight the grey sweatshirt with a mixture of 1 part

Slate Grey + 2 parts Butter Cream. Shade the yellow shirt on the girl with Raw Sienna, and highlight with a mixture of 1 part Moon Yellow + 2 parts Butter Cream. Shade the shirt on the boy in the swing with Dark Burnt Umber, and highlight with Moon Yellow. Highlight the black shirt, tire swing and leaf bag with Uniform Blue. Shade all the faces and hands with Burnt Sienna on a no. 2 flat. Paint the features with very thin, inklike Dark Burnt Umber and a no. 10/0 liner. Just paint suggestions of features. Shade the

girl's hair with Dark Burnt Umber, and highlight with Moon Yellow. Paint a few hairs with thinned Dark Burnt Umber in the shadow areas of the hair, and a few with thinned Moon Yellow in the light areas of the hair. Paint the tie around her ponytail with Butter Cream. Shade the Rookwood Red hat with a mixture of 1 part Rookwood Red + 1 part Black, and highlight with Burnt Orange. Base the rope on the swing with Raw Sienna. Shade the rake handle and the rope on the swing with Dark Burnt Umber, and highlight

with Moon Yellow. Paint the detail lines on the rope with thinned Dark Burnt Umber—these are simply connected S-strokes. Paint the soles on the black shoes and all the shoelaces with thinned Butter Cream. Highlight the prongs on the rake with very thin French Grey/Blue and a liner. Highlight the hair on all the boys with Raw Sienna. Highlight the eyes on all the children with a very tiny fleck of Butter Cream, using a liner. Stipple a few more leaves below the children, in the leaf bag and in the hands of the girl and the boy on the ground with a fuzzy no. 2 flat double-loaded with Rookwood Red and Pumpkin. Dip the tip of a liner brush into Rookwood Red and then into Pumpkin, alternating back and forth between the two puddles of paint until the color is variegated on the end of the brush. Now flick a few more leaves in the children's hands and on the ground below them. Be sure to paint out onto the border.

13 Finish the Runner

For the glow in the windows, dampen a large area with a ¾-inch (1.9cm) wash brush and clean water. Quickly float Moon Yellow at a diagonal from the top of the window down, and gently mop in all directions to soften. Paint Emperor's Gold on the inside edge of the Rookwood Red border using thinned paint and a liner. Remove any remaining graphite lines with an eraser. Apply two to three coats of waterbase varnish. Enjoy!

Project 6
SEASONAL FOUR-BIN CABINET

This four-bin cabinet takes us back in time to Grandma's country kitchen and the wonderful meals cooked there. It's great for storing flour, sugar and other baking supplies and looks great on the kitchen counter or hung on the wall. The individual bins can be removed to make it easier to paint, which is a benefit when painting a project this large.

MATERIALS

DecoArt Americana Acrylic Paints

Slate Grey DA68	Neutral Grey DA95	Charcoal Grey DA88	Taffy Cream DA5	Moon Yellow DA7	Raw Sienna DA93
Pumpkin DA13	Burnt Orange DA16	Red Iron Oxide DA96	Rookwood Red DA97	Antique Maroon DA160	True Red DA129
Winter Blue DA190	French Grey/ Blue DA98	Uniform Blue DA86	Hauser Light Green DA131	Hauser Medium Green DA132	Bright Green DA54
Mistletoe DA53	Mauve DA26	Royal Fuchsia DA151	Plum DA175	Desert Sand DA7	Khaki Tan DA173

Delta Ceramcoat Acrylic Paints

White 02505	Butter Cream 02523	Mudstone 02488	Black 02506	Wedgwood Green 02070	Dark Forest Green 02096
Chambray Blue 02514	Fjord Blue 02104	Burnt Sienna 02030	Dark Burnt Umber 02527	Materials List continued on page 79	

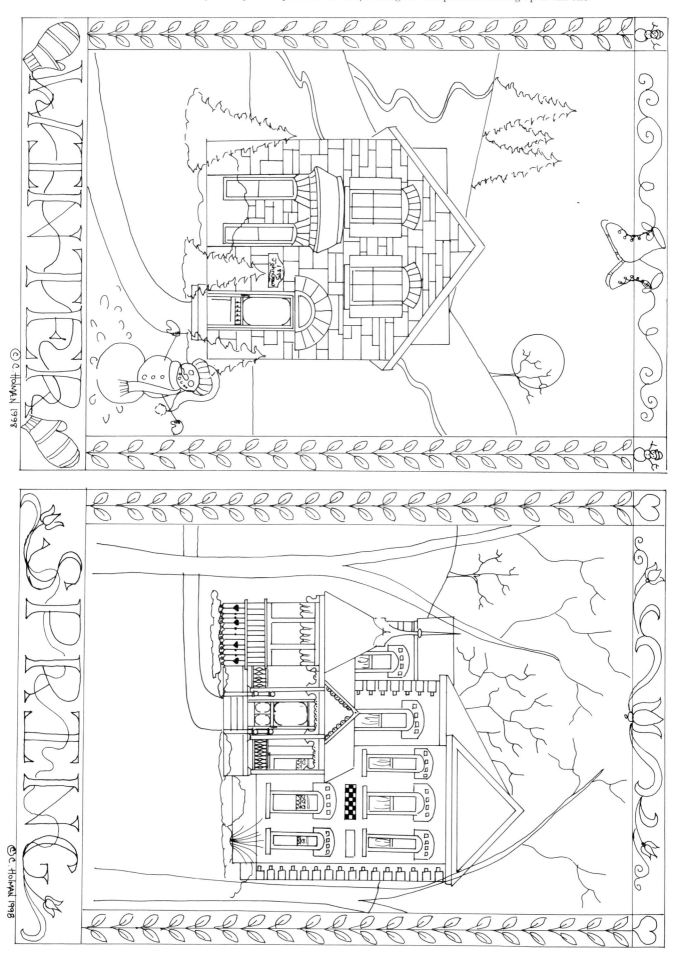

SUMMER

© C. Holman 1998

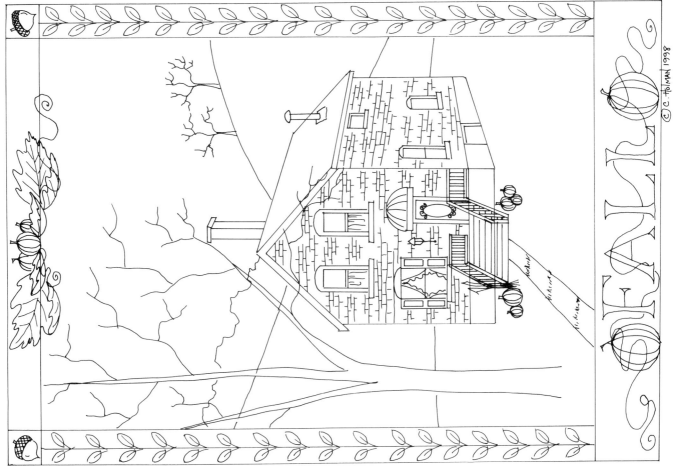

FALL

© C. Holman 1998

1 Prepare the Cabinet and Base the Borders

Seal the cabinet inside and out with wood sealer, following the directions on the bottle. When dry, sand with 400-grit black sandpaper. Using a transparent grid ruler, mark a 1″ (2.5cm) border at the bottom of each cabinet door. Apply Scotch tape above the line, and base this section with Rookwood Red, using a ¾-inch (1.9cm) wash brush. Mark a ½″ (1cm) border with the grid ruler at the top and both sides of each cabinet door. Apply Scotch tape and base this border with Khaki Tan, using a no. 10 flat brush. When the border areas are completely dry, apply Scotch tape over the painted border to keep it clean while you base-coat the sky and ground areas.

2 Paint the Fall Sky, Trees and Ground

Base the sky with Moon Yellow. Dampen the sky with a little water and use a ¾-inch (1.9cm) wash brush to float Burnt Sienna shading straight across the bottom of the sky. Walk the paint up into the sky, and quickly mop to soften. Repeat if necessary. Don't worry about being neat and keeping the Burnt Sienna off the ground area; when you base the ground, it will cover any paint that got into this area.

Solidly stipple the distant tree foliage with Dark Forest Green, using an old, fuzzy no. 4 flat. Lightly stipple with Rookwood Red and then with Burnt Orange. With Pumpkin, lightly repeat the stippling at the top of the foliage. Paint the two trees on the right at the top of the hill with a liner and Dark Burnt Umber.

Base the ground with Hauser Medium Green. Transfer the main lines for the house and the lines separating the hills. Shade the back two hills at the bottom with a ¾-inch (1.9cm) wash brush and Dark Forest Green.

Highlight the top of each hill with Hauser Light Green, using a ¾-inch (1.9cm) wash brush. (The above steps are shown completed on page 95.)

3 Base the Fall House

To base each house, use brushes that will fill the area with the least amount of strokes. Using a brush that's too small leaves ridges in the paint. Apply several thin coats of paint, until opaque. Base the right side of the house and chimney with Rookwood Red. Base the front of the house and the front of the chimney with Antique Maroon. Base the roof with Slate Grey. Base the roof trim on the front of the house with Uniform Blue and the roof trim on the side of the house with a mixture of 1 part Uniform Blue + 1 part Black. A no. 2 round works great for narrow areas such as the roof trim. Base the foundation on the right side of the house with Mudstone, and on the front of the house with a mixture of 2 parts Mudstone + 1 part Dark Burnt Umber. Base the steps with Black. Paint the brick mortar lines on

Basecoat the fall house.

Shade and base the details.

MATERIALS CONT

Loew Cornell Brushes
- Series 7300 nos. 10/0, 0, 1, 2, 4, 6, 10 and 16 flat shaders
- Series 7550 ¾-inch (1.9cm) wash brush
- Series 275 ¾-inch (1.9cm) mop brush
- Series 7000 no. 2 round
- Series 7350 no. 10/0 liner (short)
- Jackie Shaw no. 10/0 liner
- Assorted sizes of old, fuzzy flats for stippling

Other Supplies
- Designs From the Heart wood sealer
- Stain of your choice
- 1-inch (2.5cm) sponge brush
- 400-grit black wet/dry sandpaper
- Odorless turpentine
- Tracing paper
- White and gray graphite paper
- Transparent grid ruler
- Scotch Magic Transparent Tape
- J.W. etc. Right-Step matte waterbase varnish
- Magic Rub eraser

Surface
This 31″ × 12″ × 8″ (79cm × 30cm × 20 cm) wooden cabinet is available from:
Steph's Folk Art Studio
2435 Old Philadelphia Pike
Smoketown, PA 17576
(717) 299-4973

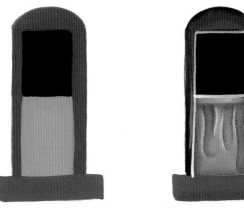

The front upper windows.

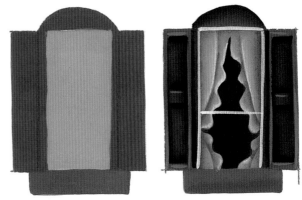

The front lower window.

the house and chimney with thinned Mudstone and a no. 10/0 liner. Shade under the ledge at the top of the chimney and under the roof on the front and side of the house with a mixture of 1 part Antique Maroon + 1 part Black.

4 Add Detail to the Fall House
Base the entire window and door areas with Uniform Blue. Always base the window and door areas with the window and door trim color. This will give you much straighter basecoating than trying to paint the trim color around the window. Base the window ledges the same color as the foundation on that side of the house: Use Mudstone on the right side of the house and a mixture of 2 parts Mudstone + 1 part Dark Burnt Umber on the front ledges. Using Fjord Blue, shade the roof with a no. 16 flat, paint the shingle lines with a no. 10/0 liner and

thinned paint and float the edges of the rocks on the foundation. The rocks are easier to paint freehand than to trace from the pattern.

5 Paint the Upper Front Windows
Base the curtain area of the two upper windows with Slate Grey and a brush that fits the width of the curtain; paint it in one stroke. Paint the upper part of the window with the same brush using Black. Shade the curtain with Fjord Blue, using a no. 6 flat for the sides and bottom of the curtain and a no. 2 flat for the gathers. If you don't like using a no. 2 flat to float, simply paint the gathers with a liner. Highlight the curtains with a no. 2 flat and Butter Cream. Outline the window and paint the center sash line with a liner and thinned Butter Cream. Shade the Uniform Blue areas with a mixture of 1 part Uniform Blue + 1 part Black. Strengthen some of this shading

with Black. Highlight with thinned French Grey/Blue and a liner. Shade the bottom of the ledge below the window with a no. 4 flat and Fjord Blue.

6 Paint the Lower Front and Side Windows
Base the inside area of the front window with Slate Grey and the area between the curtains with Black. Fill the side windows with Black. Using Fjord Blue, shade the curtains at the top and down both sides of the front window with a no. 4 flat, and the straight edge of the ruffle with a no. 2 flat. Float the highlight on the curved edges of the ruffles with Butter Cream. Outline the window and paint the center sash line with thinned Butter Cream and a liner. Shade all four sides of the panels on the shutters with a no. 2 flat and a mixture of 1 part Uniform Blue + 1 part Black. Strengthen some of this shading with Black. Highlight to the outside of

the panels with thinned French Grey/ Blue and a liner. Shade the top curve and next to the shutters on the center window section on the blue area with the Uniform Blue + Black mix. Shade and highlight the Uniform Blue areas on the side windows as instructed on page 79. Shade the bottom of all window ledges with a no. 4 flat and Fjord Blue.

7 Paint the Door
Paint the door with Butter Cream using a brush the width of the door. Shade the top of the door with a no. 6 flat and Fjord Blue. Base the oval window on the door with a small flat and Slate Grey. Shade all the way around the edges inside the oval with Fjord Blue. Float the curtain gathers with Butter Cream and a no. 2 flat. Paint the trim around the oval with thinned Rookwood Red and a no. 10/0 liner. Shade the Uniform Blue areas with a darker value of this color (mix with Black), and strengthen some areas with Black. Highlight on the opposite side of the shadows with Butter Cream. Paint the door handle with Black.

8 Finish the Fall Scene
Paint the glass section of the lantern to the left of the door with a wash of Butter Cream. Base the remainder of the lantern with Black using a liner brush. Add additional shading under the window ledges and under the outer corners of the canopy above the door with a mixture of 1 part Antique Maroon + 1 part Black, using a no. 6 flat. Paint the flashing at the bottom of the stovepipe with a mixture of 2 parts Butter Cream + 1 part Slate Grey. Shade the left edge of the flashing with Fjord Blue, and highlight the right edge with Butter Cream. Base the stovepipe with Black and highlight with French Grey/ Blue. Paint the edges of the steps and the railing with a mix of 2 parts Dark Burnt Umber + 1 part Khaki Tan. Shade the steps and railing with a mixture of 3 parts Dark Burnt Umber + 1 part Black. Highlight the steps and railing with a liner brush and Raw Sienna. Base the sidewalk with Mudstone. Shade the edges of the sidewalk with Fjord Blue. Shade to the outside of the sidewalk, on the grass, with Dark Forest Green. Flick tiny blades of grass on the sidewalk and throughout the lower ground area with Dark Forest Green and a liner. Paint the cornstalks at the end of the railing with Raw Sienna and a liner. Repeat with Moon Yellow. Paint the tie holding the stalks to-

gether with Raw Sienna. Shade below the tie with Dark Burnt Umber. Base all pumpkins with Burnt Orange. Shade all the pumpkins at the bottom and between overlapping pumpkins with Rookwood Red. Highlight the top of each pumpkin with Pumpkin. Paint the lines on the pumpkins with thinned Antique Maroon. Paint the stems with Black. Shade under the pumpkins on the ground with Dark Forest Green. Base the tree to the left of the house with Dark Burnt Umber, using a flat brush for the trunk and a liner for the branches. Shade the left side of the trunk with Black. Highlight the right side of the trunk with Raw Sienna. Stipple the leaves on the tree, those falling from the tree and the leaves on the ground with an old, fuzzy no. 2 flat double-loaded with Rookwood Red and Pumpkin.

Shade all four sides of the scene next to the border by wetting, floating and mopping with a ¾-inch (1.9cm) wash brush and Dark Burnt Umber. (The above steps are shown completed on page 95.)

9 Paint the Summer Sky, Trees and Ground
Apply tape to the border to keep it clean, and base the sky with Winter Blue. Base the sun with Moon Yellow. Shade the lower area of the sun with a ¾-inch (1.9cm) wash brush and Burnt Sienna. Paint the trunks and branches on the three trees in front of the sun with Dark Burnt Umber. Stipple the foliage heavily with Dark Forest Green. Stipple again lightly with Mistletoe and again with Bright Green, stippling more heavily on the left of each tree.

Base the ground with Dark Forest Green, and shade the bottom of the top two hills with a ¾-inch (1.9cm) wash brush using a mixture of 1 part Dark Forest Green + 1 part Black. Highlight the top of all three ground areas with Mistletoe, using a ¾-inch (1.9cm) wash brush. (The above steps are shown completed on page 94.)

The door.

10 **Base the Summer House**
Base the brick areas of the house and chimney that face forward with Rookwood Red, and the areas that face to the side with Antique Maroon. Base the siding area and roof trim below the porch roof with Taffy Cream. Base the roof areas with a mixture of 4 parts Neutral Grey + 1 part Plum. Base the roof overhang on the front and the side with a mixture of 2 parts Taffy Cream + 1 part Neutral Grey. Base the corner brick trim that faces the right side of the house with Mudstone, and all remaining corner brick trim on the front with Desert Sand. Base the top of the porch floor with the mix for the roof, and the edge of the porch with Black. Base all remaining roof trim with Taffy Cream.

11 **Add Detail to the Summer House**
Paint the brick mortar lines on the house and chimney with thinned Mudstone and a no. 10/0 liner. Shade the brick areas under the roof, to the outside of the chimney on both sides and under the ledge at the top of the chimney with a mixture of 1 part Antique Maroon + 1 part Black. Drybrush a

few of the bricks with this shading mix, using a no. 10/0 flat or a no. 2 round flattened. Using Neutral Grey on a no. 6 flat, shade the roof overhang and the top of the brick corner trim below the roof. Shade the Taffy Cream areas with Mudstone. Thin this color to paint the lap siding lines, using a no. 10/0 liner. Paint the arched bracket above the porch post with Taffy Cream, and outline along the upper curve of the arch and the right edge of the porch post with a mixture of 1 part Taffy Cream

+ 1 part Mudstone. The bracket on the other side of the porch can't be painted until the door is finished. Paint the brick mortar lines on the corner brick trim with a thinned mixture of 1 part Mudstone + 1 part Dark Burnt Umber. Shade the outside of the center peaked roof, to the left of the chimney and both ends of the porch roof with a mixture of 2 parts of the base color (Neutral Grey + Plum mix) + 1 part Black. Thin this mix to paint the shingles lines, using a no. 10/0 liner.

Base the summer house using brushes that fit the areas you are painting. Apply several thin coats.

Add shading and details.

12 Paint the Windows

Base the right section of the large front bay window with a mixture of 1 part Taffy Cream + 1 part Mudstone. Base the left and center sections of the bay window with Taffy Cream. Base the window above the bay window and the brick area below it with Desert Sand. Base the entire window on the right side of the house with Mudstone. Using a mixture of 3 parts Neutral Grey + 1 part Plum, base the roof over the bay window. Add a touch of Black to the mix to shade this roof and to paint the shingle lines. Paint the trim above the roof on the bay window with Mudstone.

Base the inside area of all windows with Neutral Grey on a no. 6 flat. Shade all windows at the top and right with Black on a no. 6 flat. Base the longer bricks on the window above the bay window using a no. 0 flat and Desert Sand. Paint the mortar lines on the brick around the windows and the brick below the bay window with a mixture of 1 part Mudstone + 1 part Dark Burnt Umber. Paint the trim around all the windows and the pane lines with thinned Taffy Cream. Shade the bay window area below the roof trim, above and below the ledge at the bottom and the arches above the windows with Mudstone.

13 Paint the Door

Base the top section of the door with Desert Sand and the door with Butter Cream. Base the windows on the door with Neutral Grey on a no. 6 flat. Shade the windows at the top and right with Black on a no. 6 flat. Using a liner, paint the gingerbread trim on the door with thinned Butter Cream and the door handle with Black.

The bay window.

The front door.

14 **Finish the Summer Scene**
Base the sidewalk with Desert Sand, and shade with Mudstone on the edges. Solidly stipple the bushes below the house with a mixture of 1 part Dark Forest Green + 1 part Black. Stipple the bushes lightly with Dark Forest Green, then Mistletoe and then at the tops with Bright Green. Paint the fern below the house with a liner and Mistletoe, then repeat with Bright Green. Paint some grass blades along the bottom edge of the sidewalk and through the sidewalk with Dark Forest Green. Repeat with Mistletoe. Also paint some grass throughout the lower ground area with Mistletoe. Base the tree to the left of the house with Dark Burnt Umber, and shade the left side with Black. Highlight the right side with Raw Sienna. Stipple the foliage on the tree and the flower foliage below the tree with a mixture of 1 part

Dark Forest Green + 1 part Black. Stipple the foliage on the tree again with Mistletoe and then again with Bright Green. Paint the flower foliage below the tree with thinned Mistletoe and a no. 10/0 liner. Repeat with Bright Green. Stipple the flowers with an old, fuzzy no. 0 flat with Pumpkin on one corner of the brush and Burnt Sienna on the other. Shade inside all four sides of the scene next to the border with a ¾-inch (1.9cm) wash brush and Dark Burnt Umber.

15 **Paint the Spring Sky, Trees and Ground**
Base the sky with Chambray Blue. Shade the lower area of the sky with Mauve, using a ¾-inch (1.9cm) wash brush. Paint the tree trunk and branches for the tree on the hill with Dark Burnt Umber. Stipple the foliage with Plum, and repeat with Royal Fuch-

sia. Base the ground with Wedgwood Green. Shade the bottom of the hill with Dark Forest Green. Highlight the top of the ground with a mixture of 1 part Wedgwood Green + 2 parts Moon Yellow. (The above steps are shown completed on page 93.)

16 **Base the Spring House**
Base the dark area below the porch roof with a mixture of 2 parts Dark Burnt Umber + 1 part Red Iron Oxide. Base the remaining brick areas with Red Iron Oxide. Base the roofs with 3 parts Neutral Grey + 1 part Plum. Base the front edge of the porch floor with Neutral Grey. Base the foundation with Mudstone and the steps with Slate Grey. Also base the sidewalk with Slate Grey. Base the remaining roof trim and the gazebo area with Butter Cream.

Base the spring house, using brushes that fit the area you're painting.

17 Add Detail to the Spring House

Shade between each brick section of the house and below the roof trim on the brick areas using a no. 10 flat and Dark Burnt Umber. Paint the brick mortar lines on the Red Iron Oxide areas with thinned Mudstone. Drybrush a few of the bricks with Dark Burnt Umber and a no. 10/0 flat. Shade the dark area below the porch roof with Black and a no. 10 flat. Base the corner brick trim with Desert Sand, using a no. 2 flat for the wider section and a no. 10/0 flat for the narrow part. Shade the roof with a mixture of 2 parts of the Neutral Grey + Plum base mix + 1 part Black. Thin this mixture to paint the shingle lines, using a liner. Base the spire at the top of the gazebo with Butter Cream. Shade the Butter Cream areas with Slate Grey and repeat with Fjord Blue, using a brush that fits the area you're shading. Paint the siding lines on the gazebo with thinned Slate Grey. Shade the steps and the foundation with Fjord Blue.

18 Paint the Windows

Base the crown above the windows and the window below the porch roof with Desert Sand. Base the remainder of all windows with Butter Cream. Base the inside area of all windows with Neutral Grey. Shade the top and the right side of the grey area in each window with Black. Paint the curtains in the windows with a wash of Butter Cream. Shade all the curtains on the brick areas of the house and float the gathers with Fjord Blue. Paint the trim on the lower lace curtains with thinned Butter Cream and a no. 10/0 liner. Add the dots at the bottom with a liner. Paint the pane lines in the windows with thinned Butter Cream. Shade the crown at the top of the windows with Mudstone and a no. 6 flat. Paint the red bricks on the crown above each window with a no. 10/0 flat and Red Iron Oxide. Shade the cur-

Add shading and details.

The upper windows.

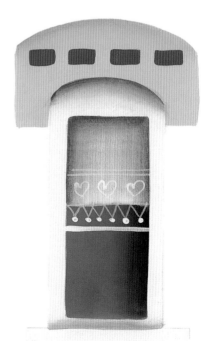

The lower windows.

tains on the gazebo windows at the top and down both sides with Fjord Blue. Float the folds with Fjord Blue. Drybrush the center of each fold (gather) with a no. 2 round and Butter Cream.

19 Paint the Door

Base the entire door area with Desert Sand. Fill the door with Raw Sienna. Base the inside area of the window and the screen area on the door with Neutral Grey. Shade the top and right side of the window and screen with Black. Paint the screen lines and the door handle with thinned Black. Paint the remaining gingerbread trim on the screen door with Raw Sienna and a liner.

20 Finish the Spring Scene

Base the porch railing, porch posts and the gingerbread trim with Butter Cream. Paint the stone between the upper and lower windows on the far right with Mudstone, and shade with Fjord Blue. Paint the center checkerboard area on the bricks with Red Iron Oxide. Paint every other check with a mixture of 1 part Red Iron Oxide + 1 part Black. Shade the top and both sides of this checkerboard area with this same mix. Shade all remaining Butter Cream areas with Slate Grey, then shade again with Fjord Blue. Shade the Desert Sand areas with Mudstone. Add a tiny black dot in each curve of the gingerbread trim with a liner. Using thinned Black, outline along the top edge of the peak on the house and porch roofs. Paint the lines, hearts and dots on the lower gazebo area with thinned Black. Outline the top of each porch step with Butter Cream. Stipple the flower foliage and bushes below the house with a mixture of 1 part Dark Forest Green + 1 part Black. Stipple the foliage again with a mixture of 1 part Dark Forest Green + 1 part Wedgwood Green. Paint the branches on the bush on the right with Wedgwood Green, and repeat with a

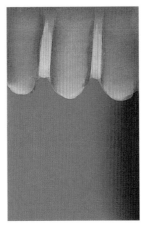

The gazebo windows.

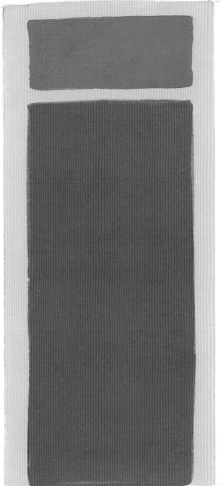

The front door.

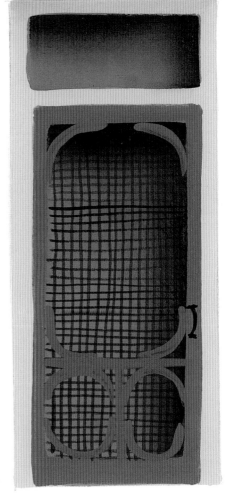

mixture of 1 part Wedgwood Green + 2 parts Moon Yellow. Stipple the flowers below the house with a fuzzy no. 0 flat double-loaded with Plum and Royal Fuchsia. Shade the sidewalk with Fjord Blue, and shade to the outside of the path with Dark Forest Green. Paint a few blades of grass along the edge of the sidewalk and throughout the lower ground area with thinned Dark Forest

Green and a liner. Paint the trees on each side of the house and the branches behind the house with thinned Dark Burnt Umber. Shade the trees with Black, and highlight with Raw Sienna. Stipple foliage very lightly with Dark Forest Green. Shade all four sides of the scene next to the border with a ¾-inch (1.9cm) wash brush and Dark Burnt Umber.

21 Paint the Winter Sky, Trees and Ground

Base the sky with Uniform Blue and the ground with French Grey/Blue. Highlight the top of the hills with a mixture of 2 parts White +1 part French Grey/Blue, using a ¾-inch (1.9cm) wash brush. Shade between the hills with a mixture of 2 parts Uniform Blue + 1 part French Grey/Blue, using a ¾-inch (1.9cm) wash brush. Shade the paths on the hills and the sidewalk below the house with this same mix. Float to the outside of the paths and the sidewalk with the highlight mix (White + French Grey/Blue). Base the moon with Butter Cream. Highlight the top and left side of the moon with White. Shade the right side with French Grey/Blue.

Heavily stipple all the evergreen trees on the hill with Black. Stipple lightly all over with French Grey/Blue, leaving a shadow between the trees. Repeat with a mix of 1 part French Grey/Blue + 1 part White, and once again with White on the right side of the trees. Base the tree in front of the moon with Dark Burnt Umber, and paint some snow on the branches with the French Grey/Blue + White mix. (The above steps are shown completed on page 92.)

22 Base the Winter House

Base the roof with Neutral Grey. Base the main area of the house with Desert Sand. Base the roof trim with Butter Cream. Base the roof overhang and the steps with Mudstone.

23 Add Detail to the Winter House

Shade the Desert Sand area of the house with Mudstone, using a no. 16 flat. Base the entire window and door areas, the trim below the bay window roof and the sign with Butter Cream. Base the shutters and the bay window roof with Black. Using a no. 10 flat, shade the Neutral Grey roof sections with Black above the Butter Cream roof trim. Paint the stone mortar lines with thinned Butter Cream. Drybrush each stone with a little Charcoal Grey, using a no. 1 or no. 2 flat. Shade the main area of the house once again with a mixture of 1 part Mudstone + 1 part Charcoal Grey. Also shade the overhang on the roof and the steps with this mix, using a no. 4 flat. Shade the Butter Cream areas with Fjord Blue, using a no. 6 flat.

Base the winter house.

Add shading and details.

24 Paint the Windows

Base the inside area of the dark windows with Neutral Grey and the lit windows with Moon Yellow, using a brush the width of the windows. Shade the grey windows at the top and left with Black, using a no. 10 flat. Shade the yellow windows at the top and left with Burnt Sienna, again using a no. 10 flat. Paint the pane lines in the windows with thinned Butter Cream. Shade the top curve on the Butter Cream trim, next to the shutters, and above the window ledges with a no. 6 flat and Fjord Blue.

25 Paint the Door

Shade the panel below the screen area on the door with Fjord Blue. Outline the top and both sides of the door with thinned Fjord Blue on a liner. This goes between the door and the door frame. Shade the top and left side of the screen area with Black on a no. 10 flat. Shade the top and left side of the yellow window with a no. 4 or no. 6 flat and Burnt Sienna. Paint the screen lines on the grey area of the door with thinned Black on a liner. Paint the gingerbread trim on the door with thinned Butter Cream and a liner, and add dots with a stylus. The glow from the window is floated on in step twenty-seven.

26 Paint the Snowman

Base the snowman's body with French Grey/Blue on a no. 6 flat. Highlight the left side of each section of the body with a mixture of 1 part French Grey/Blue + 1 part White on a no. 10 flat. Shade the top of each section of the body with a no. 6 flat and Uniform Blue. Float a shadow on the ground to the right of the snowman with Uniform Blue. Base the hat and scarf with Rookwood Red on a no. 2 flat, and the cuff on the hat with Dark Forest Green. Shade the hat and scarf with a mixture of 1 part Rookwood Red + 1 part Black and highlight with True Red, using a no. 4 flat. Highlight the

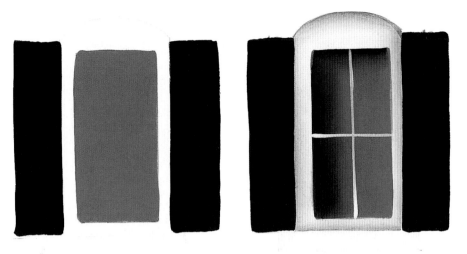

The dark windows.

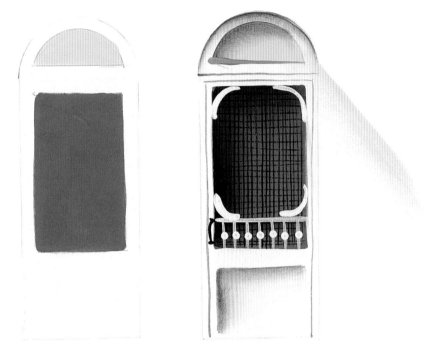

The front door.

The large snowman.

left side of the snowman's body again with Moon Yellow. Paint the arms with a liner and Dark Burnt Umber. Base the gloves with Dark Forest Green. Shade the cuff on the hat and the gloves with a mixture of 1 part Dark Forest Green + 1 part Black and highlight with Mistletoe, using a no. 4 flat. Paint the ribbing on the cuff of the hat with thinned Mistletoe and a liner. Paint the eyes, mouth and buttons with Black on a liner (don't dot them with a brush handle or stylus), and highlight with a fleck of Butter Cream. Base the nose with Burnt Orange, using a liner, and shade along the bottom of the nose with Rookwood Red, using a no. 2 flat or liner. Float a shadow under the nose with a no. 2 flat or a wash of Uniform Blue and a liner. Stipple the ball on the end of the hat with a fuzzy no. 2 flat double-loaded with Fjord Blue and Butter Cream. Add touches of snow on the hat, nose, arms and gloves with a liner and the French Grey/Blue + White mix. Highlight the left end of the cuff on the hat with Moon Yellow. Float the footprints in the snow at the base of the snowman with a no. 2 flat and a mixture of 3 parts Uniform Blue + 1 part French Grey/Blue. Highlight to the outside of the footprints with the lighter French Grey/Blue + White mix.

27 Finish the Winter Scene
Outline along the peak of the roof and the sign with Black. Paint the lettering on the sign, the screen lines on the door and the door handle with thinned Black and a no. 10/0 liner. Highlight the black roof above the bay window with French Grey/Blue.

Heavily stipple the trees and bushes below the house with Black. Stipple lightly with French Grey/Blue, then with a mixture of 1 part French Grey/Blue + 1 part White and once again with a little White where the light from the windows would shine on the trees. Also tap a little Moon Yellow on

the trees in the same areas you stippled with White. Wet, float and mop the glow from the yellow windows with a no. 16 flat. With a mix of 1 part French Grey/Blue + 1 part White, paint a little snow on the steps, windowsills, the lower part of the fan window, roof and the top of the sign, using a liner brush. Wet, float and mop the glow from the yellow windows with a no. 16 flat and Moon Yellow. Shade all four sides of the scene next to the border with Dark Burnt Umber and a ¾-inch (1.9cm) wash brush.

28 Paint the Fall Border
Paint the squares in the two upper corners with Black. Paint the lettering on the lower border with a no. 2 flat and Black, using shape-following strokes as in calligraphy. Paint the narrow lines on the lettering with thinned paint and a liner. Paint the vine lines on the lower border around the pumpkins and lettering with Hauser Medium Green and a liner. Base the pumpkins on the top border with a no. 4 flat and Burnt Orange. Follow the instructions in step eight to complete all of the pumpkins. Shade under the pumpkins on the lower border with a mixture of 1 part Antique Maroon + 1 part Black. Base the two large leaves on the

top border with Antique Maroon and a no. 4 or no. 6 flat. Shade above the fold and along the bottom edge of the fold with a no. 6 flat, using a mixture of 1 part Antique Maroon + 1 part Black. Highlight these leaves with Burnt Orange along the ruffled edge of the fold on the leaf and the top ruffled edge of the leaf. Thin the shading mix to paint the veins, using a liner. Highlight the veins in a few places with thinned Burnt Orange and a liner. Base the two smaller leaves with Raw Sienna and a no. 2 flat. Shade the leaves with a mixture of 1 part Raw Sienna + 1 part Dark Burnt Umber. Highlight the leaves with a mixture of 1 part Moon Yellow + 1 part Raw Sienna. Paint the veins on these leaves with a mix of 1 part Raw Sienna + 1 part Dark Burnt Umber. Highlight the veins in a few places with a mixture of 1 part Moon Yellow + 1 part Raw Sienna and a liner. Thin some Raw Sienna + Dark Burnt Umber mix to paint the vines. Highlight the vines where they cross over the dark leaves with a mixture of 1 part Moon Yellow + 1 part Raw Sienna, using a liner. Paint the acorns inside the black squares with Khaki Tan. Base the cap on the acorn and the stem with a mixture of 1 part Raw Sienna + 1 part

Base the pumpkins and leaves on the top border.

Shade, highlight and add vines.

Dark Burnt Umber. Shade all the edges of the acorn with a mixture of 1 part Khaki Tan + 1 part Dark Burnt Umber. Highlight the center of the nut part of the acorn with Butter Cream. Shade the cap on the acorn on both ends with Dark Burnt Umber. Highlight the center of the cap with Raw Sienna. Shade under the cap once again with Dark Burnt Umber. Paint the detail on the cap with thinned Raw Sienna and a liner. Shade the stem where it attaches to the cap with Dark Burnt Umber.

29 Paint the Summer Border

Paint the squares in the upper corners with Black. Base the lettering on the lower border with Black, using a no. 2 flat and a liner. With Moon Yellow, base the centers of the daisies with a no. 2 round. Also use Moon Yellow to base the sun. Shade the bottom curve of the flower centers with Burnt Sienna, and float a tiny C-stroke in the center. Shade the bottom of the sun's face with a no. 6 flat and the sun rays and eyes with a no. 2 flat, again using Burnt Sienna. Paint the daisy petals with a liner and Butter Cream. Paint S-stroke daisy leaves with a no. 2 flat double-loaded with Mistletoe and Dark Forest Green. Shade the sun again with Dark Burnt Umber. Highlight the top curve of the sun with a no. 6 flat and on the opposite side of the shading in the center of each sun ray with a no. 2 flat and Taffy Cream. Highlight the

eyes on the sun with a couple of flecks of Butter Cream, using a liner. Base the birds with French Grey/Blue. Shade below the wings on the birds with Uniform Blue on a no. 4 flat, and shade below each tail feather with a no. 2 flat. Highlight the birds with Winter Blue on a no. 4 flat. Float the lower edge of each tail feather with a no. 2 flat and Winter Blue. Float a little Butter Cream on the lower portion of the stomach next to the tail. Float Rookwood Red on the chest and stomach. Paint the beak, eye and feet with Black and a liner. Highlight the eye with a fleck of Butter Cream. Paint the scrolls with a liner and thinned Dark Forest Green. Paint the vine on the lettering on the lower border with Mistletoe.

Base the sun and birds on the top border.

Shade, highlight and add details.

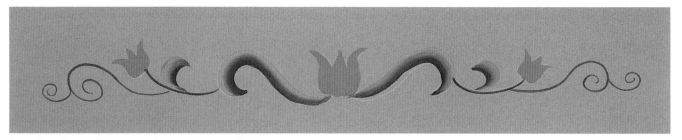

Base the tulips and leaves on the top spring border.

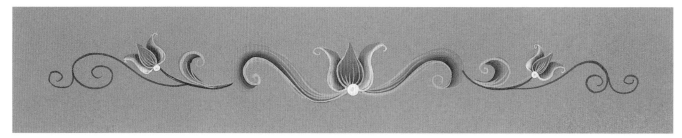

Highlight, shade and add liner work.

30 **Paint the Spring Border**
Paint the squares in the upper corners and the lettering on the lower border with Black, using a no. 2 flat. Paint the tulips and hearts on the border with Mauve and a no. 2. Highlight the outer edge of the two outside petals on the tulips and the hearts with Butter Cream. Shade next to the center petal and at the bottom of the center petal with Plum. Paint the liner detail on the tulips with thinned Butter Cream. Paint the tulip leaves with a double-loaded no. 2 flat, using Dark Forest Green and Wedgwood Green, keeping the light color at the top. Paint the scrolls with a liner and thinned Dark Forest Green. Paint the liner detail on the leaves with a mixture of 2 parts Butter Cream + 1 part Wedgwood Green. Use the handle end of a liner for the dot on the center top tulip and the large end of a stylus for the dots on the small tulips.

31 **Paint the Winter Border**
Paint the squares in the upper corners of the border and base the lettering on the lower border with Black. Base the gloves on the lower border with Dark Forest Green, and shade with a mixture of 1 part Dark Forest

Green + 1 part Black. Highlight the gloves and paint the ribbing lines on the cuff of the glove with Mistletoe. Paint the stripes on the gloves with Rookwood Red and highlight the center of each stripe with True Red, using a liner. Paint the string for the gloves with Mistletoe.

Base the skates in the top border with Butter Cream, using a no. 6 flat. Shade with French Grey/Blue and deepen the shading inside the top of the skates and where the heels cross

over with Fjord Blue, still using a no. 6 flat. Paint the shoelace holes and the blades with Black on a liner, and highlight the blades with a liner and French Grey/Blue. Paint the shoelaces with thinned Butter Cream and a no. 10/0 liner. Base the tiny snowmen in the upper corners with French Grey/Blue. Highlight the left of the bodies with a mix of 1 part French Grey/Blue + 1 part White. Shade with Uniform Blue at the top of each section of the body. Base the hat and scarf with Rook-

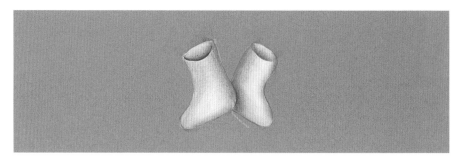

Base and shade the skates on the top border.

Highlight and add details.

wood Red, and shade with a mixture of
1 part Rookwood Red + 1 part Black.
Highlight the hat and scarf with True
Red. Base the arms with a mixture of 1
part Dark Burnt Umber + 1 part
Khaki Tan. Paint a little snow on the
arms with a mix of 1 part French Grey/
Blue + 1 part White. Paint the eyes,
mouth and buttons with Black, and
highlight with a fleck of Butter Cream.
Paint the nose Burnt Orange.

32 Finish the Cabinet

After you have painted all four
scenes, paint the vines on the border of
the doors with a wash of Dark Forest
Green, using a liner for the stems and
a no. 4 flat for the leaves. Shade the
bottom curve of each leaf where it attaches to the stem with Dark Forest
Green and a no. 4 flat. Paint the detail
lines on the leaves and the leaf stems
with thinned Dark Forest Green. Create the dots at the base of the stems on
the winter border with the large end of
a stylus using Rookwood Red. On the
spring border, the dots are Dark Forest
Green. The dots on the summer border
are Moon Yellow, and the dots on the
fall border are Burnt Orange.

To finish the cabinet, stain the remainder of the cabinet, including the
bins, with your choice of stain. Use a
little odorless turpentine on a rag to remove any stain that gets onto the front
of the door. Allow to dry several days.
Remove any remaining graphite lines
with a Magic Rub eraser, and apply
two to three coats of waterbase varnish.

Paint the vines on
the borders after you
have completed all
four scenes.

SEASONAL FOUR-BIN CABINET

Project 7
GARDEN CABINET

This curved-front cabinet could be used for multiple purposes, but since I painted it with a Victorian garden theme, I've decided to use it for small garden tools, gloves, seed packets and small pots. I photographed the Victorian home in Lexington, Missouri, a town where I have taken several photos of old Civil War-era homes. If you decide you like painting architecture, always carry a camera on trips. This is a great way to gain a wealth of information on different home types, and you'll be surprised at the vast array of painting sources you can accumulate.

MATERIALS

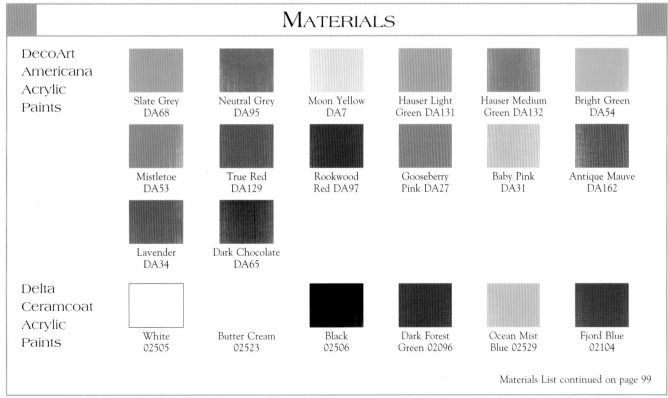

DecoArt Americana Acrylic Paints					
Slate Grey DA68	Neutral Grey DA95	Moon Yellow DA7	Hauser Light Green DA131	Hauser Medium Green DA132	Bright Green DA54
Mistletoe DA53	True Red DA129	Rookwood Red DA97	Gooseberry Pink DA27	Baby Pink DA31	Antique Mauve DA162
Lavender DA34	Dark Chocolate DA65				

Delta Ceramcoat Acrylic Paints					
White 02505	Butter Cream 02523	Black 02506	Dark Forest Green 02096	Ocean Mist Blue 02529	Fjord Blue 02104

Materials List continued on page 99

This pattern may be hand-traced or photo-copied for personal use only. Enlarge pattern at 189 percent to bring up to full size.

©C. Holman 1998

Loew Cornell Brushes
- Series 7300 nos. 10/0, 0, 1, 2, 4, 6, 10 and 16 flat shaders
- Series 7550 ¾-inch (1.9cm) wash brush
- Series 275 ¾-inch (1.9cm) mop brush
- Series 7000 no. 2 round
- Series 7350 no. 10/0 liner (short)
- Jackie Shaw no. 10/0 liner
- Assorted sizes of old, fuzzy flats for stippling

Surface
This 24½″ × 14¼″ × 8⅛″ (62cm × 36cm × 21cm) curved-front wooden cabinet is available from:
Sechtem's Wood Products
533 Margaret St.
Russell, KS 67665
(785) 483-2960

Other Supplies
- 1-inch (2.5cm) sponge brush
- Burnt Umber oil paint
- Odorless turpentine
- Tracing paper
- White and gray graphite paper
- Scotch Magic Transparent Tape
- Paper towels
- Designs From the Heart wood sealer
- 400-grit black wet/dry sandpaper
- J.W. etc. Right-Step matte waterbase varnish
- Magic Rub eraser
- Styrofoam tray

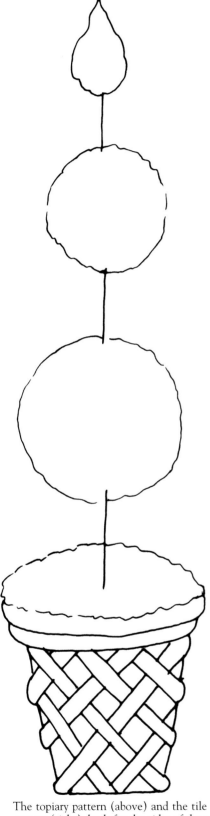

The topiary pattern (above) and the tile pattern (right), both for the sides of the cabinet, may be hand-traced or photocopied for personal use only. Both appear here at full size.

1 Prepare the Cabinet

Seal the entire cabinet, inside and out, with Designs From the Heart wood sealer, following the directions on the bottle. Sand with 400-grit sandpaper. Trace your pattern onto tracing paper. Base the entire cabinet, except the front of the door, with Black.

2 Paint the Sky, Ground and Trees

Base the sky with Ocean Mist Blue. Dampen the sky with a ¾-inch (1.9cm) wash brush and clean water, and stipple the clouds with Butter Cream on an old, fuzzy no. 16 flat. Quickly mop to soften. Allow to dry and repeat these same steps on the upper edges of the clouds, using White.

Base the ground area with Dark Forest Green. Stipple the grass with Hauser Medium Green, and repeat with Hauser Light Green at the top of the ground area. Transfer the main lines for the house. Base the tree trunk to the right of the house with Dark Chocolate. Heavily stipple the tree foliage behind the house to the right with Dark Forest Green. Stipple again with Mistletoe and repeat with Bright Green, stippling more heavily at the top of the foliage. (The above steps are shown completed on page 104.)

3 Base the House

Base the brick areas of the house with Rookwood Red, using a brush that fits the area you're working on. Base the foundation and trim areas with Butter Cream. Base the roof sections and the steps with Neutral Grey. Apply several thin coats to achieve a smoother basecoat. Shade the Rookwood Red areas with a floated mixture of 1 part Rookwood Red + 1 part Black.

Base and shade the additional details.

Base the house and shade the Rookwood Red areas.

4 Base the Details and Add More Shading

Now transfer the outer trim lines for the windows, doors, porch roof trim and posts by the doors. Base these areas with Butter Cream. Add a little more shading below some of these areas and to the outsides of the turret on the first and second floor with the Rookwood Red + Black mix.

Shade the Butter Cream areas with Slate Grey. Shade the vertical rows of bricks on the tower with a mixture of 1 part Rookwood Red + 1 part Black.

5 Complete the House

Shade the Butter Cream areas with Slate Grey, and strengthen some of this shading with Fjord Blue. Use a no. 4 flat and a no. 2 flat for the tinier floats, such as in the door. Starting at the top of the shaded trim area under the upper roof overhang, paint the dentil (notched) molding with a no. 2 flat and Butter Cream. Shade along the top

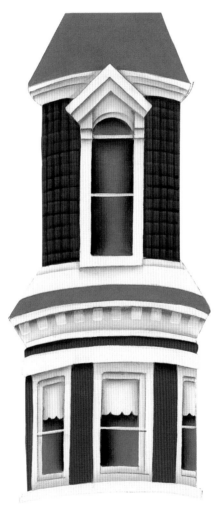

Shade the bottom and highlight the top of each row of bricks on the tower. Deepen some of the shading on the Butter Cream areas with Fjord Blue. Paint the dentil molding notches with Butter Cream, and shade the top of each notch with Fjord Blue. Base the inside area of the windows with Fjord Blue and shade with Black. Paint the pane lines in all the windows with thinned Butter Cream.

of each notch with Fjord Blue on a no. 2 flat. Base the inside area of all windows with Fjord Blue. Float Black shading in all the Fjord Blue windows. Paint a thin line of Black along the top edge of the two peaked porch roofs. Using a no. 2 flat, shade the right side of the vertical rows of bricks on the tower to the left of the window, and the left side of the rows to the right of the window, with a mixture of 1 part Rookwood Red + 1 part Black. Highlight the top of each of these decorative bricks with True Red and a no. 2 flat. Shade the bottom of each row of bricks with the shading mix. Add linework detailing on the porch roof trim in the inset areas and on the door panels with thinned Fjord Blue. Paint the sheer curtains in some of the windows with a wash of Butter Cream. Float the curtain folds with Butter Cream, using a no. 4 flat. Paint the floral design on the curtains with thinned Butter Cream, using a no. 10/0 liner. Paint the pane lines in all the windows with thinned Butter Cream. Paint the brick mortar lines on the Rookwood Red areas of the house with a thinned mixture of 1 part Rookwood Red + 1 part Black. Base the remaining posts and railing with Butter Cream. Shade with Slate Grey and repeat with Fjord Blue. Paint all the gingerbread trim and the weather vane with Butter Cream. Paint the cutout areas in the gingerbread trim with Fjord Blue. Paint the lattice circles in the area below the porch with Black and a no. 10/0 liner. Paint the door handles with Black, using a liner. Shade the roof and the steps with a mixture of 1 part Neutral Grey + 1 part Black. Thin this mix to paint the shingle lines on the roof areas, using a liner. Shade below and on the left of some of the shingles with this same mix and a no. 6 flat. Highlight the bottom of some of the shingles with Slate Grey.

6 Paint the Sidewalk, Flowers and Fence

Base the sidewalk with Rookwood Red, and shade with 1 part Rookwood Red + 1 part Black. Thin this mix to paint the mortar lines, using a liner. Stipple grass onto the edges with a fuzzy no. 6 flat and Dark Forest Green, then with Hauser Medium Green and finally with Hauser Light Green. Heavily stipple the flower foliage below the house with 1 part Dark Forest Green + 1 part Black. Repeat with Dark Forest Green, Mistletoe and Bright Green. Paint the dark flowers at the base of the foliage on every other clump with a fuzzy no. 2 flat double-loaded with Antique Mauve and Baby Pink. Paint the lighter flowers at the base with a double-loaded brush, using Butter Cream and Baby Pink. The little yellow daisies have Butter Cream centers and Moon Yellow petals—paint these with a liner. The lavender daisies have Moon Yellow centers and Lavender petals. Shade the bottom of the yellow centers with Rookwood Red.

Paint the fence with Black and a liner. Highlight the fence with thinned Ocean Mist Blue, using a liner. Float this color on the two posts by the gate. Stipple the flower foliage below the fence using the same colors as you used for the foliage below the house. Paint the stems for the coral bells at the top of the foliage with thinned Mistletoe and Bright Green. Using a fuzzy no. 0 flat, stipple the coral bells on these stems with Gooseberry Pink on one corner and Butter Cream on the other. Stipple the flowers at the base of the foliage with a fuzzy no. 0 flat double-loaded with Moon Yellow and Lavender. Base the flowerpots on the steps with a mixture of 3 parts Gooseberry Pink + 1 part Rookwood Red. Shade the flowerpots with Rookwood Red. Paint the topiary trunks in the pots with Dark Chocolate. Stipple the topiaries on the steps with Dark Forest Green, Mistletoe and Bright Green. Paint the vine up the left side of the building with a liner and Mistletoe. Paint the tree limbs above the house on the left with thinned Dark Chocolate. Stipple the foliage on these limbs very lightly with Dark Forest Green.

Shade the top and left side of the inset panels on the door with Slate Grey.

Strengthen some of the shading with Fjord Blue. Paint the detail in the panels and circle trim with thinned Fjord Blue and a liner. Base the transom window with Slate Grey, and shade the top and both ends of this window with Black before you paint the scalloped trim that hangs over it. Shade the scalloped trim with Slate Grey and then Fjord Blue. Shade below where this trim crosses over the outer edges of the door. Paint the door handles with Black and a liner.

Base all windows with Fjord Blue and shade with Black.

Paint the curtains over the windows with a very light wash of Butter Cream, using a brush that fits the width of the window. When the wash is dry, float the folds in the curtains with Butter Cream and a no. 4 flat. Paint the floral design on the curtains with thinned Butter Cream and a liner.

7 Paint the Border and the Sides of the Cabinet

Base a 2″ (5cm) border at the bottom of the door with Black. Use tape to keep the upper edge straight. Base the tiles in the corner of the border and the tiles on the sides of the cabinet with Slate Grey. Shade the tile designs with Fjord Blue, and highlight with Butter Cream. Base the watering cans with Slate Grey, shade with Fjord Blue and highlight with Butter Cream. Base the flowerpots on the border and sides with 3 parts Gooseberry Pink + 1 part Rookwood Red. Carefully transfer the weaving pattern, and shade to the outside of each strip of weaving and the outer edges of the flowerpot with a no. 6 flat and Rookwood Red. Highlight the rims of the pots with 2 parts Gooseberry Pink + 1 part Butter Cream. To highlight the center of each woven strip with the same mix, dampen with water, applying a little paint with a liner and quickly mop. Do only one section at a time. Paint the topiary trunks with Dark Chocolate. Stipple all the foliage on the topiaries with Dark Forest Green. Lightly stipple the foliage in the pot with Hauser Medium Green. Stipple the remaining foliage with Mistletoe and once again with Bright Green, stippling more heavily at the top and left of each section. Base the trunk with Dark Chocolate, and shade at the top and left side of each section with Black. Shade the bottom of the trunk coming out of the pot with Black. Paint the vine topiaries with a liner, using Mistletoe and Bright Green. Paint the liner detail on the border by the pots and the strokes below the pots on the sides of the cabinet with Mistletoe. The water sprinkling up out of the cans are dashes of thinned Slate Grey. Shade the lower ground area above the border with a ¾-inch (1.9cm) wash brush and Dark Chocolate. Base the tassels and draped strokes at the top of the cabinet sides with Slate Grey, and shade with Fjord Blue. Base the top and bottom edges of the cabinet with Rookwood Red.

Base the tiles with Slate Grey. Float Fjord Blue shading on the design.

Highlight the design with Butter Cream. The easiest way to achieve this is to dampen the area with a little water, tap a little paint in the highlight area with a liner and quickly but gently mop in all directions to soften. Work only one area at a time.

Base the watering cans with Slate Grey, and shade with floated Fjord Blue.

Highlight the watering can with Butter Cream. Dampen the area, apply the paint with a liner and quickly mop to soften.

Base the flowerpot with the Gooseberry Pink + Rookwood Red mix, and shade with Rookwood Red. Heavily stipple foliage with Dark Forest Green. Lightly stipple foliage on the spheres with Mistletoe.

Highlight the flowerpot. Base and shade the topiary trunk and stipple the topiary spheres with Bright Green and the foliage in the pot with Hauser Medium Green.

❧ Charming Village Scenes You Can Paint ❧

8 Antique the Cabinet

Remove all remaining graphite with an eraser or with turpentine on a paper towel. Mix Burnt Umber oil paint and odorless turpentine in a Styrofoam tray. With a sponge brush, apply this antiquing glaze over the entire door area, on the sides of the cabinet and over the Rookwood Red edges of the cabinet. Remove all excess antiquing with paper towels. To remove more antiquing from the center of the painted areas, use a paper towel dampened with turpentine. Keep removing and blending the antiquing, keeping it darker in the corners and around the edges. Allow to dry several days, then varnish with several coats of waterbase varnish. Time to garden!

Project 8

UMBRELLA STAND

S oft, gentle rain evokes thoughts of spring with budding trees, tulips, rainbows and kids splashing in puddles. What an amazing time of year! It's like a cleansing of the mind and soul. If you live in an area where you don't have much use for an umbrella stand, this also makes a great fern stand. So, if the rain is gently beating against your windows and you can't get outside to work in the garden, why not paint a place to rest your umbrella?

MATERIALS

DecoArt Americana Acrylic Paints					
Slate Grey DA68	Neutral Grey DA95	Moon Yellow DA7	Antique Gold DA9	Raw Sienna DA93	Blue Mist DA178
French Grey/ Blue DA98	Uniform Blue DA86	Black Green DA157	Rookwood Red DA97	Black Plum DA172	Medium Flesh DA102
Khaki Tan DA173					

Delta Ceramcoat Acrylic Paints					
White 02505	Butter Cream 02523	Black 02506	Wedgwood Green 02070	Dark Forest Green 02096	Rainforest Green 02462
Leaf Green 02067	Periwinkle Blue 02478	Fjord Blue 02104	Burnt Sienna 02030	Dark Burnt Umber 02527	

Materials List continued on page 108

Loew Cornell Brushes
- Series 7300 nos. 10/0, 0, 1, 2, 4, 6, 10, 12 and 16 flat shaders
- Series 7550 ¾-inch (1.9cm) wash brush
- Series 275 ¾-inch (1.9cm) mop brush
- Series 7000 no. 2 round
- Series 7350 no. 10/0 liner (short)
- Jackie Shaw no. 10/0 liner
- Assorted sizes of old, fuzzy flats for stippling

Other Supplies
- 1-inch (2.5cm) sponge brush
- Transparent grid ruler
- Styrofoam tray
- Palette knife
- Designs From the Heart wood sealer
- 400-grit black wet/dry sandpaper
- Paper towels
- Krylon Matte Finish spray #1311
- Burnt Umber oil paint
- Odorless turpentine
- Tracing paper
- White and gray graphite paper
- Scotch Magic Transparent Tape
- J.W. etc. Right-Step matte waterbase varnish
- Bubble wrap (preferably 1″ [2.5cm] bubbles)
- Magic Rub eraser

Surface
This 26½″ × 8½″ (67cm × 22cm) wooden umbrella stand is available from:
Sechtem's Wood Products
533 Margaret St.
Russell, KS 67665
(785) 483-2960

This pattern may be hand-traced or photo-copied for personal use only. Enlarge at 200 percent, then again at 107 percent to bring it up to full size.

© C Holman 1998

1 Prepare the Umbrella Stand and Paint the Sky and Ground

Seal and sand the entire piece, inside and out, following the directions on the bottle of sealer. Mark a 1" (2.5cm) border at the top and bottom on all four sides of the stand for the checkerboard area. Trace the pattern onto tracing paper, and apply the pattern for the top of each ground or hill area using gray graphite paper.

Base the sky with Blue Mist and a ¾-inch (1.9cm) wash brush. Again using the ¾-inch (1.9cm) wash brush, base the top left hill with a mixture of 1 part Wedgwood Green + 1 part Butter Cream. Working your way down from the top, base the next ground area with Wedgwood Green, then the next one down with a mixture of 1 part Wedgwood Green + 1 part Dark Forest Green and the bottom section with Dark Forest Green. Highlight the top of each ground area by wetting, floating and mopping with a ¾-inch (1.9cm) wash brush, working your way down from the top hill. Highlight the top left hill with a mixture of 5 parts Butter Cream + 1 part Wedgwood Green. Highlight the next hill with a mixture of 1 part Butter Cream + 1 part Wedgwood Green, then the third hill down with Wedgwood Green and the bottom hill with a mixture of 1 part Wedgwood Green + 1 part Dark Forest Green.

Shade the bottom of each hill with a ¾-inch (1.9cm) wash brush. Float the top left hill with Wedgwood Green, the next hill with a mixture of 1 part Wedgwood Green + 1 part Dark Forest Green, the third hill with Dark Forest Green and the bottom hill with Black Green. Shade the bottom of all the ground areas again with a value darker than you used the first time, in order from top to bottom: 1 part Wedgwood Green + 1 part Dark Forest Green, Dark Forest Green, 1 part Dark Forest Green + 1 part Black Green, and finally Black.

Base the sky and ground starting with the top and working your way down to the bottom. Apply two to three coats of paint until the coverage is opaque.

Wet, float and mop the highlight at the top of each ground section using a lighter value than the basecoat.

Shade the bottom of each ground using a darker value than the basecoat. Strengthen each shaded area once again with an even darker value.

2 Paint the Sun and Clouds

Base the sun with Moon Yellow and a no. 10 flat. Shade the sun with Raw Sienna, using a no. 4 flat for the smaller floats on the rays and the facial features and a no. 16 flat for the float across the lower area of the face. Strengthen this shading again with Dark Burnt Umber. Highlight the sun on the opposite side of the shading on each ray, around the curve of the sun and along the left side of the nose with a mixture of 1 part Butter Cream + 1 part Moon Yellow. With a liner, add tiny flecks of Butter Cream in the upper left and lower right of the iris.

With clean water and a ¾-inch (1.9cm) wash brush dampen a larger area than your clouds will actually cover. Stipple the clouds with an old, fuzzy no. 10 flat and Butter Cream, then quickly mop to soften. Repeat this step once again to make the clouds more opaque. Wet, stipple and mop the bottom of each cloud with Fjord Blue, using a fuzzy no. 6 flat (or you can simply load half of your no. 10 fuzzy flat). Highlight the top of each cloud using the same technique and White. If you lose too much of the base color, allow the cloud to dry thoroughly, then repeat this step by stippling the Butter Cream back in the center of the cloud.

3 Paint the Rainbow and Trees

The rainbow is based with washes of color (thin each color with water), using a no. 2 flat or a no. 2 round. Paint the top stripe with Moon Yellow, the second stripe with Periwinkle Blue, the third stripe with Dark Forest Green and the fourth stripe with Rookwood Red. Shade the bottom of the yellow stripe with Raw Sienna, the blue stripe with Uniform Blue, the green stripe with Dark Forest Green and the red stripe with Rookwood Red, using a no.

4 flat for each. Shade the ends of the rainbow where they disappear behind the hills with Dark Burnt Umber and a no. 12 flat. Shade the top of the sky with a ¾-inch (1.9cm) wash brush and Dark Burnt Umber. Base the tree trunks on the two small trees at the top of the hills with Dark Burnt Umber. Stipple the foliage on these two trees very lightly with a fuzzy no. 4 flat and Dark Forest Green.

4 Paint the Distant House

Base the distant house behind the hill with Butter Cream and the roof with Black. Base the chimney with Rookwood Red. Shade below the roof with Fjord Blue and a no. 6 flat. Base the window with Black. Shade the bottom of the chimney with a mix of 1 part Rookwood Red + 1 part Black on a no. 2 flat. Outline the window and paint the pane lines with thinned Butter Cream and a no. 10/0 liner. High-

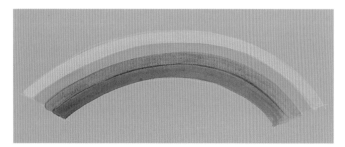

Base the sun with Moon Yellow and shade with Raw Sienna. Wet, stipple and mop the clouds. Allow the cloud to dry completely, and then repeat the same step.

Strengthen the shading on the sun and add highlights. Wet, stipple and mop the shading at the bottom of the cloud. Highlight the top of the cloud using the same technique.

Make a wash of each of the rainbow colors by adding water with your brush to the edge of a puddle of paint until the paint is transparent. Don't try to thin the whole puddle of paint. Blot the excess water out of your brush and then load into the wash and base the stripes. If your wash is too light, add more paint; if it's too dark, add more water.

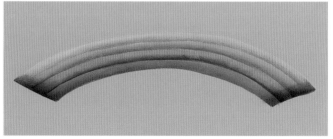

Shade the lower curve of each stripe with floated color. Shade the ends of the stripes with a float of Dark Burnt Umber.

light the top of the roof with Periwinkle Blue and a no. 6 flat.

5 Paint the Road, Fence and Large Tree

Base the road with Khaki Tan, and shade with Dark Burnt Umber. Flick grass along the edges of the road with a liner and thinned Dark Forest Green. Paint the fence with Dark Burnt Umber and a liner. Stagger grass here and there throughout the ground areas with thinned Dark Forest Green. Base the large tree by the road with Dark Burnt Umber. Shade the left side of the tree trunk with Black. Stipple the foliage lightly with Dark Forest Green. Flick some grass around the base of the tree with Dark Forest Green and repeat with Wedgwood Green. (This step is shown completed on page 115.)

6 Paint the Schoolhouse

Base the front of the school with Rookwood Red and the side with Black Plum. Base the roof, including the roof of the bell tower, with Black. Also base the bell with Black. Base the front of the bell tower with Butter Cream, and the side with a mixture of 1 part Butter Cream + 1 part Slate Grey. Base the top of the steps and the flagpole with the grey mix, and the risers and ends of the steps with Slate Grey. Base the flag with Butter Cream. Paint the blue field of the flag with Uniform Blue, and the stripes with a liner and Rookwood Red. Float shading down the left side of the flagpole with Fjord Blue and highlight the opposite side with thinned Butter Cream and a liner. Shade the left side of the blue field of the flag with Black and a no. 4 flat, and both ends of the stripes with Fjord Blue and a no. 4 flat. The stars are tiny Butter Cream Xs. Shade under the roof on the side and front of the school with a no. 6 flat and a mixture of 1 part Black Plum + 1 part Black. Shade the bottom of each Slate Grey area of the steps with Fjord Blue. Shade the bell tower on the light grey and Butter Cream areas with Fjord

Base the distant house with a brush that fits the area you are working in.

Detail the distant house.

Base the school with brushes that fit the areas you are working on. Base the entire flag with Butter Cream first, and then paint the blue and red over the top.

Thin paint to an inklike consistency for the liner detailing on the windows, sign, roof trim and the detail on the bell tower. Stipple the bushes and paint the flowers with a double-loaded brush; you may use any two-color combinations from the palette if you prefer.

Blue. Paint the liner detailing on the tower with thinned Fjord Blue. Base the door and sign with Butter Cream and a no. 8 flat. Paint the windows with Fjord Blue, using a no. 2 flat for the window above the door and a no. 10 flat for the other windows. Shade the windows at the top and left with Black and a no. 4 flat. Shade the top of the door and the sign with Fjord Blue and a no. 4 flat. Paint a thin line of Fjord Blue down the center to divide the two doors. Dot the doorknobs with Black. Outline the windows and

paint the pane lines with thinned Butter Cream and a liner. Outline along the edge of the roof with the Butter Cream. Highlight the roof areas with a no. 10 flat and Periwinkle Blue. Also highlight the bell with Periwinkle Blue. Heavily stipple the bushes below the school with Dark Forest Green, and repeat lightly with Wedgwood Green. Stipple the flowers at the bottom of these bushes with a fuzzy no. 10/0 flat double-loaded with Periwinkle Blue on one corner of the brush and Moon Yellow on the other.

7 Paint the Children

Paint the puddles below the children's feet with a wash of Blue Mist. Float the outer edges of the puddles with the same color. Base the faces, hands and legs on the children with Medium Flesh and brushes that fit the areas you are painting. Base the yellow raincoat, boots and umbrella with Moon Yellow. Base the blue umbrella, hat and coat with Periwinkle Blue. Base the hair on the girl in yellow with Raw Sienna. Shade the flesh areas with Burnt Sienna and a no. 2 flat. Most of the shading and highlighting on the clothes can be done with no. 2 and no. 4 flats. Shade the yellow areas with Raw Sienna. Strengthen the Raw Sienna shading with Burnt Sienna. Shade the hair with Dark Burnt Umber. Shade the blue areas with Uniform Blue. Paint the ripple lines in the puddles and the water splashing up from the feet with thinned Butter Cream and a liner. Paint the handles on the umbrellas and the little peak at the top of the umbrella with Black, and highlight with thinned Butter Cream and a liner. Paint a Slate Grey dot at the end of the points on the umbrellas, and highlight with Butter Cream. Highlight all the Moon Yellow areas with Butter Cream, and the blue areas with a mixture of 1 part Periwinkle Blue + 1 part Butter Cream. Paint the lines on the blue umbrella with thinned Uniform Blue and on the yellow umbrella with thinned Raw Sienna.

8 Paint the Pond

Base the pond with Blue Mist and a no. 16 flat. Shade the pond with a mixture of 1 part Blue Mist + 1 part Uniform Blue. Base the bank along the upper edge of the pond with Khaki Tan on a no. 2 round, and shade with Dark Burnt Umber and a no. 2 flat. Dampen the entire pond with clean water using a ¾-inch (1.9cm) wash brush, and float a back-to-back highlight in the center of the pond with

Paint the puddles with a transparent wash of Blue Mist. Base the children with brushes that fit the areas you're working on.

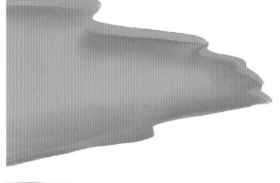

Add details to the children and puddles.

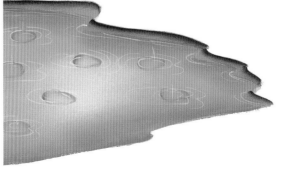

Base the pond with Blue Mist. Shade the upper and lower edges of the pond by wetting, floating and mopping a darker value.

Highlight the center of the pond with Butter Cream. If you have a problem with back-to-back floating, you could dampen the area, stipple the highlight in the center of the pond and quickly mop.

Butter Cream, walking the color out a little to the right and the left. Quickly mop in all directions to soften. Float the ripples in the pond with the shading mix. Each ripple is done with two floated C-strokes. Float a C-stroke on the left and then the right, with the color fading to the center of the oval. Add thinned Butter Cream ripple lines around the outside of these floats. Add raindrops with a liner hitting in the center of each oval. Also, add ripples along the upper edges of the water where it splashes against the bank.

9 **Base and Shade the Large House** Base the main area of the large house with Khaki Tan and a ³⁄₄-inch (1.9cm) wash brush. Base the roof area with Fjord Blue and a no. 10 flat. Base the trim at the top of the roof with Neutral Grey and a no. 2 round. Base the trim below the roof with Butter Cream and a no. 4 flat. Shade the Fjord Blue area of the roof with Black. Base the window areas on the roof with Butter Cream on a no. 4 flat, and the trim at the top of these windows with Neutral Grey and a no. 2 round. Shade all the Neutral Grey trim at the top of the roof with 1 part Neutral Grey + 1 part Black and a no. 2 flat. Paint the tiny arches on the tower roof trim with a liner and Butter Cream. Shade the Khaki Tan area of the house with Neutral Grey and a no. 10 flat, then thin this color to paint the lap siding lines using a no. 10/0 liner.

10 **Complete the House** Now transfer the pattern for the remaining windows, door, porch roof, posts and other details. Base the remaining windows, porch posts, railing, door and gingerbread trim with Butter Cream, using brushes that fit the area you are painting. Base the porch roof with Fjord Blue, and the trim at the top and bottom of the Fjord Blue areas with Neutral Grey. Also paint the outside trim of the triangular area with Neutral Grey and a no. 2

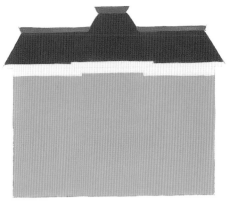

Base the large house.

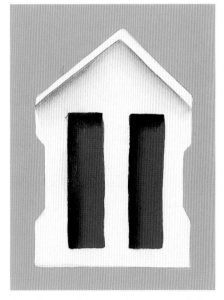

Base the remaining window areas with Butter Cream. Shade with Fjord Blue close to the tops of these areas. Base the windows with Fjord Blue. Shade the top and left side of each window with Black.

round. Paint the center triangle with Rainforest Green. Base the porch floor trim and the steps with Slate Grey. Base the area below the porch floor trim with Fjord Blue, and then paint Black over the top with a no. 2 flat for the lattice area. Outline below the Butter Cream trim at the top of the house with the Rainforest Green. Shade under the Butter Cream porch roof trim with Neutral Grey. Shade all the Butter Cream and Slate Grey areas with Fjord Blue. Shade the Fjord Blue roof area with Black, and the Neutral Grey trim with 1 part Black + 1 part Neutral Grey. Shade the Rainforest Green triangle with Fjord Blue and a

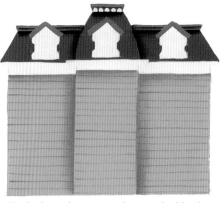

Shade, base the top windows and add siding lines.

Paint the curtains with a liner and Butter Cream. Shade the top and left side of the curtains with Fjord Blue. Paint the remaining trim with thinned Rainforest Green.

no. 2 flat.

Base the door with Raw Sienna and a no. 10 flat. Paint all the windows with Fjord Blue and a no. 2 flat. Shade the top and left side of all the Fjord Blue windows with Black and a no. 2 flat. Paint the railing at the top of the roof with a liner and thinned Black. Highlight the black railing with thinned Periwinkle Blue. Paint the curtains with Butter Cream and a liner. Shade the curtains with Fjord Blue and a no. 2 flat. Outline around the windows and paint the decorative trim above and between the windows with thinned Rainforest Green and a no. 10/0 liner. Shade the door along the top and down both sides with Dark Burnt Umber. Also shade to the inside of the panel designs on the doors to make them recede. Highlight the raised areas of the door with Antique Gold. Thin this color and outline around the windows on the door. Paint the handles with dots of Black. Outline along the triangular peak on the porch roof with Black and a liner. Paint the shine marks on the windows with dashes of thinned Butter Cream and a no. 10/0 liner. Paint a line of thinned Butter Cream down the edges of the house. Paint the cutouts on all the gingerbread trim with Fjord Blue and a liner. Paint the dentil (notched) molding on the Butter Cream trim at the top of the house with a no. 10/0 flat and Neutral Grey. Paint the lattice over the Black area at the bottom of the porch with thinned Butter Cream and a liner. Paint the black areas of the lanterns by the door with a liner, and the center glass area with a wash of Butter Cream. Highlight the black lantern areas with thinned Periwinkle Blue. Shade next to the window trim on the upper roof with Black. Heavily stipple the trees and bushes below the house with Black. Stipple again lightly with Dark Forest Green. Stipple all these areas again, except the rounded bush at each corner of the house, using a mixture of 1 part Dark Forest Green + 1 part Wedgwood Green. Stipple the rounded bushes at the corners of the house with Leaf Green. Paint the tulip foliage and stems at the bottom of the house with Leaf Green and a liner. Paint the tulips with 1 part Rookwood Red + 1 part Butter Cream.

11 Paint the Umbrellas and Tulip Design

Base the foreground umbrellas with Black and the handles with Raw Sienna. Paint the metal point at the top of the umbrella and the dots on the bottom tips with Slate Grey. Paint the tulip with a no. 2 flat double-loaded with Butter Cream on one corner of

the brush and a mixture of 1 part Butter Cream + 1 part Rookwood Red on the other. Blend the brush back and forth on the palette in a sweeping motion, carefully staying in the same streak. Paint the outer petals of the tulip first, using an S-stroke, and then the center petal. Shade to the right of the center petal with a float of Rookwood Red. Paint the stem with Leaf Green and a liner brush. Paint the tulip leaves and remaining strokes at the bottom with a no. 4 flat double-loaded with Leaf Green and a mixture

of 1 part Dark Forest Green + 1 part Leaf Green. Add a Leaf Green dot at the base of the tulip. Paint the remaining liner scrolls with thinned Leaf Green. Shade the handles on the umbrella with Dark Burnt Umber, and highlight with Antique Gold. Highlight the black areas of the umbrellas with Periwinkle Blue. Shade the grey areas of the umbrellas with Fjord Blue, and highlight with Butter Cream. Paint the rain dashes all over the scene with a liner and thinned Butter Cream.

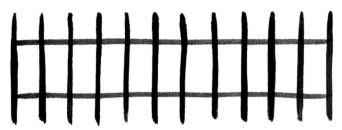

Paint the main railing lines at the top of the porch roof and the top of the tower with thinned Black and a no. 10/0 liner.

Add as much or as little detail to the railing as you like. Embellish with dots of black. Highlight here and there with any of the light blues in the palette, using thinned paint and a liner.

Add details to complete the house.

12 Finish the Umbrella Stand

Base the sides and the back of the umbrella stand with Rookwood Red. Tape off and paint the checkerboard area first with Butter Cream. Using a transparent grid ruler, mark ½" (1cm) squares, and base every other check with Black, using a no. 12 flat. Protect the molding at the top and bottom of the stand with paper towels or a rag, and lightly spray all four sides of the stand with Krylon Matte Finish spray. With a palette knife, mix Burnt Umber oil paint and odorless turpentine in a Styrofoam tray. This antiquing glaze should be dark but easy to spread. Apply the antiquing with a sponge brush over the checkerboard and the red sides of the stand, antiquing one side at a time. Lay bubble wrap on top of the antiquing and press. You can press once for a uniform design or lift the wrap and repeat to get a completely different look. With a paper towel wrapped around your index finger, blend the antiquing on the checkerboard areas.

Dampen the entire side of the stand with the painted scene with a paper towel blotted with odorless turpentine. With a dry paper towel wrapped around your finger, apply a little oil paint to the outer edges of the scene. With another dry paper towel, gently blend the antiquing into the scene. (Don't use the paper towel blotted with turpentine to blend because it will take off all the oil paint.) If you aren't satisfied with the results, simply remove the oil paint with turpentine and start over. Apply the antiquing to the molding at the top and bottom of the stand, and remove the excess. Allow to dry one to two days, and then paint some of the molding trim with Dark Forest Green. Remove any remaining graphite lines with a Magic Rub eraser, and apply two to three coats of varnish. Now that the rain's over, go out and enjoy the sunshine!

Project 9
MEET ME AT THE GARDEN GATE

What better way to accent a room than with the warm glow of a hand-painted lamp. This design would look lovely in any room of the house. Gardening is one of my newest passions and seems to be working its way into several of my projects lately. I've always found that gardeners make great painters—I truly hope the reverse will turn out to be true! This pattern would also fit a flat surface, if you prefer.

MATERIALS

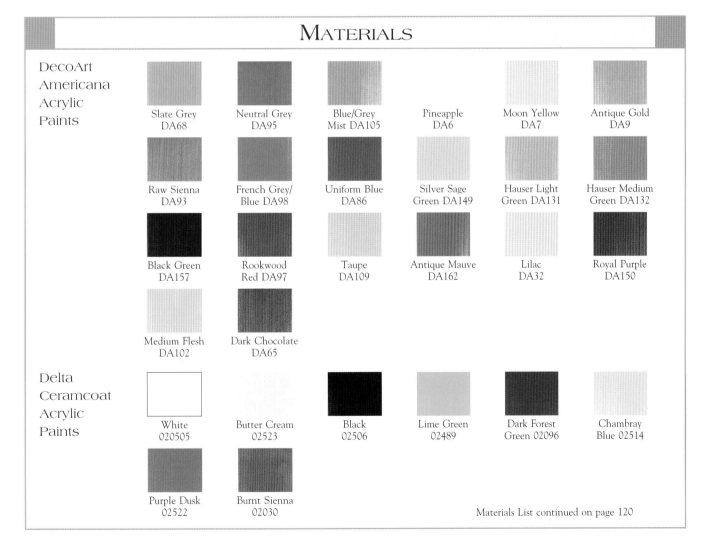

DecoArt Americana Acrylic Paints

Slate Grey DA68	Neutral Grey DA95	Blue/Grey Mist DA105	Pineapple DA6	Moon Yellow DA7	Antique Gold DA9
Raw Sienna DA93	French Grey/Blue DA98	Uniform Blue DA86	Silver Sage Green DA149	Hauser Light Green DA131	Hauser Medium Green DA132
Black Green DA157	Rookwood Red DA97	Taupe DA109	Antique Mauve DA162	Lilac DA32	Royal Purple DA150
Medium Flesh DA102	Dark Chocolate DA65				

Delta Ceramcoat Acrylic Paints

White 020505	Butter Cream 02523	Black 02506	Lime Green 02489	Dark Forest Green 02096	Chambray Blue 02514
Purple Dusk 02522	Burnt Sienna 02030				

Materials List continued on page 120

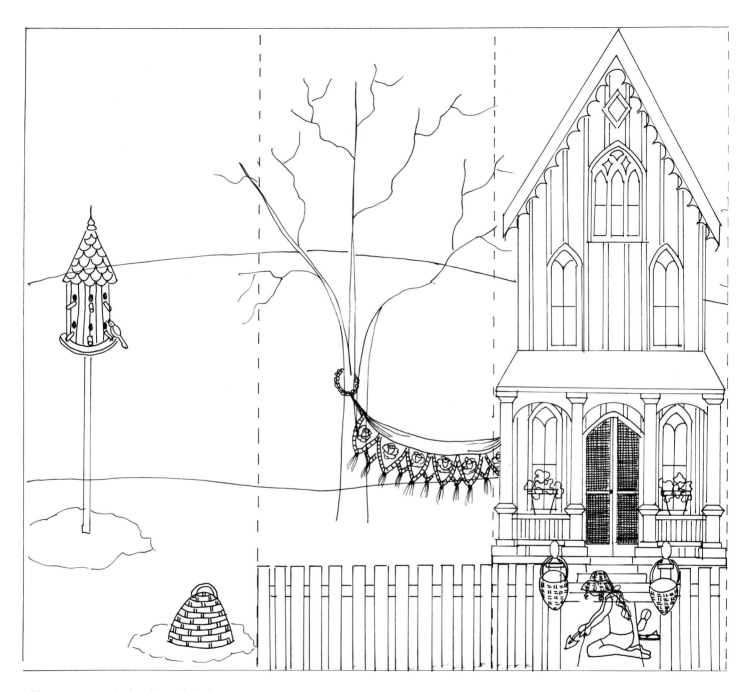

This pattern may be hand-traced or photo-copied for personal use only. Reattach right and left halves of pattern. Enlarge pattern at 141 percent to bring up to full size. Cut pattern along dotted lines. This makes the pattern easier to apply to each side of the base.

©C. Holman 1998

1 Prepare the Lamp and Base the Sky and Ground

Seal and sand the wood following the manufacturer's directions. Trace the pattern onto tracing paper and transfer the main outlines. Base the sky with Chambray Blue, using a ¾-inch (1.9cm) wash brush. Dampen the sky with clean water, again using a ¾-inch (1.9cm) wash brush. Stipple a cloud with an old, fuzzy no. 10 flat and Butter Cream, then quickly mop to soften. Repeat, adding clouds here and there on each side of the lamp. Shade the top of the sky with a ¾-inch (1.9cm) wash brush and French Grey/Blue. Base the top ground area with Hauser Medium Green. Base the lower ground area with Dark Forest Green. Shade the lower edge of the top ground area with a ¾-inch (1.9cm) wash brush and Dark Forest Green. Stipple the top ground area with Hauser Light Green, using an old, fuzzy no. 10 flat, and repeat with a brush mix of Hauser Light Green and Moon Yellow. Stipple the lower ground area with Hauser Medium Green. Stipple the top of the lower ground area once again with Hauser Light Green.

Loew Cornell Brushes
- Series 7300 nos. 10/0, 0, 1, 2, 4, 6, 10 and 16 flat shaders
- Series 7550 ¾-inch (1.9cm) wash brush
- Series 275 ¾-inch (1.9cm) mop brush
- Series 7000 no. 2 round
- Series 7350 no. 10/0 liner (short)
- Jackie Shaw no. 10/0 liner
- Assorted sizes of old, fuzzy flats for stippling

Other Supplies
- 1-inch (2.5cm) sponge brush
- Designs From the Heart wood sealer
- 400-grit black wet/dry sandpaper
- Krylon Matte Finish spray #1311
- Odorless turpentine
- Burnt Umber oil paint
- Paper towels
- Bubble wrap
- Styrofoam tray
- Palette knife
- Tracing paper
- White and gray graphite paper
- Scotch Magic Transparent Tape
- J.W. etc. Right-Step matte waterbase varnish
- Magic Rub eraser

Surface
This 12¾" (32cm) tall wooden lamp base is available from:
Sechtem's Wood Products
533 Margaret St.
Russell, KS 67665
(785) 483-2960

2 Base the House

Base the main area of the house with Silver Sage Green on a ¾-inch (1.9cm) wash brush. Base the porch roof and the porch foundation with Neutral Grey and a no. 16 flat. Using Butter Cream, base the roof trim with a no. 4 flat, the porch roof trim with a no. 2 round and the porch floor trim with a no 2 flat. Shade under the roof areas with Blue/Grey Mist, using a ¾-inch (1.9cm) wash brush. Shade on each side of the vertical siding with the same color, using a no. 6 flat to float the shading. With a little water, dampen the narrow vertical strips left between the shading. With a mixture of 2 parts Butter Cream + 1 part Silver Sage Green, quickly paint a streak along this area with a liner, then mop vertically to soften. Base the remaining trim areas, including windows, door, porch posts and other details with Butter Cream, using a brush that fits the area you are basing. Base the steps with Silver Sage Green and the sidewalk with Rookwood Red, using a no. 10 flat.

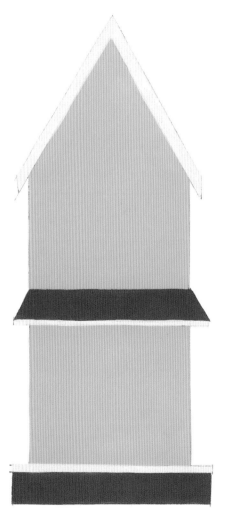

Base the house. Apply several thin coats until you have opaque coverage.

Add siding lines and base the main details.

3 Add Detail to the House

Shade all the Butter Cream areas with Slate Grey, using a no. 4 or no. 6 flat for most areas. Shade the bottom of each step with Blue/Grey Mist. Outline the top of each step with thinned Butter Cream and a liner. Base the inside area of all windows and the screen area of the door with Neutral Grey. Shade the top and left side of all the Neutral Grey areas of the windows and door with Black. Also shade the top and outside edges of the porch roof, below the porch floor trim and next to the steps with Black and a no. 10 flat. Using a wash mixture of 2 parts Butter Cream + 1 part Silver Sage Green on a no. 10 flat, paint the curtains. Float the gathers with a no. 2 flat and the same mix. Thin this mix to paint the lace designs on the curtains, using a no. 10/0 liner. Shade down both sides of the curtains with French Grey/Blue and a no. 4 flat. Paint the gingerbread trim and the windowpane lines with thinned Butter Cream and a liner. Paint the line dividing the two screen doors with thinned Black and a liner. Paint the screen lines on the door, dot the doorknob and outline along the top edge of the main roof with Black. Shade the sidewalk with 1 part Rookwood Red + 1 part Black on a no. 10 flat. Paint the brick mortar lines on the sidewalk with thinned Neutral Grey and a no. 10/0 liner. Drybrush a few of the bricks with Butter Cream, using a no. 0 flat. Stipple onto the edges of the sidewalk with Dark Forest Green, and repeat with Hauser Medium Green.

4 Paint the Bushes and Flowers Below the House

Steps four and five are shown completed on page 127. Stipple the bushes heavily with Black Green. Repeat with a brush mix of Dark Forest Green and Hauser Medium Green. At the top of the bushes, stipple lightly with Lime Green. Paint the vine up the left post on the house with Hauser Medium Green. Stipple the flowers on this vine

Complete the house.

with a fuzzy no. 0 flat double-loaded with Taupe on one corner of the brush and Antique Mauve on the other corner. Paint the large round flowers in the bushes with a fuzzy no. 2 flat double-loaded with Royal Purple and Lilac. Paint the spiky flowers with a fuzzy no. 0 flat double-loaded with Purple Dusk and Butter Cream.

5 Paint the Two Large Trees

Base the trees with Dark Chocolate. Shade the left side of the trunk with a mixture of 1 part Dark Chocolate + 1 part Black. Highlight the right side of the trunk with Raw Si-

enna. Stipple the foliage heavily with Dark Forest Green. Stipple again lightly with a brush mix of Hauser Medium Green and Dark Forest Green, and repeat with Lime Green. Stipple a little grass at the base of the trunks with Dark Forest Green, Hauser Medium Green and Hauser Light Green.

6 Paint the Fence and Flowers

Lay a piece of Scotch tape above the fence so the top of each post will be the same height. Base the fence with a no. 4 flat and Butter Cream. Use a no. 2 round for the finial. Shade the left side of each section of fence

with Slate Grey. Stipple the flower foliage at the bottom of the fence with Black Green on an old, fuzzy no. 6 flat, then with a brush mix of Dark Forest Green and Hauser Medium Green and once again with Lime Green. Paint the vines on the fence with Hauser Medium Green, and stipple these flowers with a fuzzy no. 1 flat double-loaded with Taupe and Antique Mauve. Paint the round flowers with a fuzzy no. 2 flat double-loaded with Lilac and Royal Purple. Stipple the spiky flowers with a fuzzy no. 1 flat double-loaded with Purple Dusk and Butter Cream.

Base the fence and foliage.

Stipple the foliage with several values of green. When painting the double-loaded flowers, be sure to blend the brush by tapping it up and down on the palette to soften the colors in the center.

7 Paint the Distant House

Base the front of this house with Butter Cream and the right side with a mixture of 2 parts Butter Cream + 1 part Silver Sage Green, using a brush that fits the area you're working in. Base the chimney with Rookwood Red. Base the roofs with Black. Shade under the roofs with Slate Grey, using a no. 6 flat. Base the windows with Neutral Grey. Base the door with Rookwood Red. Shade the top and the left side of all the windows with Black on a no. 4 flat. Shade the door and the chimney with a mixture of 1 part Rookwood Red + 1 part Black and a no. 2 flat. Base the shutters with Black on a no. 2 flat. Paint the remaining trim on the house with thinned Butter Cream and a no. 10/0 liner. Highlight the roof with French Grey/Blue.

8 Paint the Lady Gardening

Base the woman's face, arms and legs with Medium Flesh. Base her hat and shoes with Raw Sienna, her shirt with Butter Cream, her shorts with French Grey/Blue, her trowel with Slate Grey and her glass with a wash of Butter Cream. Base the baskets hanging from the fence posts with Raw Sienna. Shade the hat, shoes and hanging baskets with Dark Chocolate. Paint the weaving on the baskets and the woman's hat with thinned Dark Chocolate and a liner. Highlight the vertical weaving with thinned Antique Gold and a liner. Shade the shirt with Slate Grey, the shorts with Uniform Blue and the flesh areas with Burnt Sienna. Paint the thong strap on the shoes, the sole on the bottom shoe and the hatband with thinned Black. Paint the hair with a liner using thinned Dark Chocolate. Highlight the hair with a few strands of thinned Antique Gold, and paint the bow with French Grey/Blue. Shade the trowel with a mixture of 1 part Slate Grey + 1 part Black, and highlight with Butter Cream. Float the top and left side of each ice cube in the glass with White, and float White on the edges of the glass. Shade down in the opening of the glass with Slate Grey. Paint the straw with Butter Cream, and shade with a thin line of Slate Grey down the left side of the straw. Paint the stripes on the straw with Rookwood Red. Shade below the woman's legs and the glass with a mixture of 1 part Rookwood Red + 1 part Black on a no. 6 flat.

Base the distant house.

Add details.

Base the woman with small flats or a no. 2 round.

Apply the shading with a no. 2 or no. 4 flat unless otherwise indicated.

9 Paint the Flowers in the Basket and Flowerpots

Base the flowerpots on the porch railing with a mixture of 4 parts Antique Mauve + 1 part Dark Chocolate and a no. 4 flat. Shade the flowerpots with a mixture of 1 part Rookwood Red + 1 part Black, again using a no. 4 flat. Paint the leaves in the flowerpots and in the hanging baskets with a mixture of 2 parts Butter Cream + 1 part Dark Forest Green, using a liner or a no. 2 round. Shade the leaves with Dark Forest Green and a no. 2 flat. Add the detail on the leaves with a liner and thinned Dark Forest Green. Highlight the leaves with thinned Butter Cream and a liner. Paint the flower stems with the base color for the leaves. Stipple the geraniums in the flowerpots with a fuzzy no. 1 flat double-loaded with Rookwood Red and Butter Cream. Stipple the flowers in the baskets with a fuzzy no. 1 flat double-loaded with Uniform Blue and Butter Cream.

10 Paint the Hammock

Base the hammock with a thin wash of Butter Cream and a no. 10 flat. Shade with a mix of 1 part Butter Cream + 1 part Black on a no. 6 flat. Highlight the hammock on the upper edges and the left side of each large scallop with a float of Butter Cream. Paint the detailing on the hammock with thinned Butter Cream and a no. 10/0 liner. Add a dot at the top of each tassel. Paint the shadow under the hammock with a wash of Dark Forest Green.

Paint the flower baskets and base the leaves.

Detail the leaves and stipple the flowers.

Base and shade the flowerpots.

Add the leaves and geraniums.

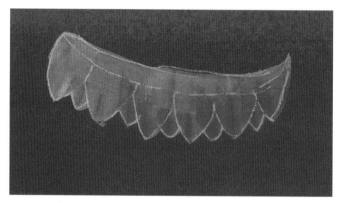

Paint the hammock with a light wash of Butter Cream.

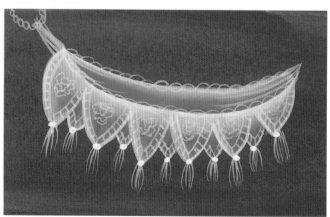

Add shading, highlights and detail.

11 Paint the Bee Skeps

Base the bee skeps at both ends of the fence with Raw Sienna on a no. 10 flat. Shade the skeps with Dark Chocolate on a no. 10 flat. To highlight, dampen the skep with clean water, float back-to-back in the center with Antique Gold and quickly mop in all directions to soften. Paint the detailing on the skeps with thinned Dark Chocolate and a liner. Highlight between the vertical weaving with a liner and thinned Antique Gold. Stipple the foliage below the skeps with a brush mix of Dark Forest Green and Butter Cream. Stipple the flowers on this foliage with a brush mix of Purple Dusk and Butter Cream.

12 Paint the Birdhouse

Base the main area of the birdhouse with Silver Sage Green, the tray with Taupe, the roof with Raw Sienna and the finial and post with Butter Cream. Shade the main area of the birdhouse below the roof and above the feeding tray with Blue/Grey Mist; thin this color to paint the vertical siding. Base the holes on the birdhouse with a liner and Black. Paint the lower edge of the feeder tray with a thinned mix of 4 parts Antique Mauve + 1 part Dark Chocolate, using a liner. Also shade the top of the Taupe area with this mix. Base the perches with Silver Sage Green and a liner. Shade below the perches with Blue/Grey Mist on a no. 2 flat, and highlight the tops with Butter Cream, using a no. 2 flat or liner. Outline the right edge of the right entrance holes, the left edge of the left entrance holes and the bottom of the center holes with thinned Butter Cream. Shade the roof below each row of shingles, below the finial and down both sides with Dark Chocolate, and highlight the lower edge of each shingle with Antique Gold. Using Slate Grey, shade on the left side of the finial with a no. 2 flat, and the top and left side of the post with a no. 4 flat. Stipple the foliage heavily at the base

Base, shade and highlight the bee skeps, and paint the horizontal weaving lines.

Paint the vertical weaving lines, and highlight between them. To paint the foliage, dip the brush into one color, tap the brush on the palette, dip into the other color and tap on the palette. The flowers are done the same way.

Base the birdhouse with brushes that fit the area you are working on.

Add the details, foliage and flowers.

of the post with Black Green. Repeat lightly with a brush mix of Dark Forest Green and Butter Cream, then stipple again with Silver Sage Green. Paint the centers of the yellow daisies with dots of White and the petals with Pineapple, using a liner. Again using a liner, paint the centers of the pink daisies with Moon Yellow and the petals with a mix of 1 part White + 1 part Antique Mauve. Paint the vine on the post with Dark Forest Green and a liner. Paint the flowers with White on a liner or no. 2 round, and float the

edges of the flowers with Purple Dusk on a no. 2 flat. Paint the centers with a dot of Antique Gold on a liner. Base the bird with Butter Cream. Apply a wash of Raw Sienna over the entire bird. Paint the top of the head with a wash of Purple Dusk. Wash the chest with Rookwood Red and the wing with Moon Yellow. Paint the detail on the feathers and the feet with a liner and a thinned mix of 2 parts Dark Chocolate + 1 part Black. Paint the eye with a dot of Black, then add a tiny fleck of Butter Cream in the center. Paint the beak with a liner and Moon Yellow, and outline to the outside of the beak with the mix of 1 part Dark Chocolate + 1 part Black.

13 Paint the Distant Trees
Base the trees with Dark Chocolate. Outline on the left side of the trunks with Black. Stipple the foliage heavily with Dark Forest Green. Repeat lightly with Hauser Medium Green and Lime Green.

14 Finish the Lamp
Apply tape all the way around the lamp at the top and bottom of the scene to protect it while basecoating the remainder of the lamp. Base the top of the lamp with Rookwood Red and the edge of the top with Dark Forest Green. Paint the top rounded edge of the base of the lamp with Dark Forest Green, and the remainder of the base with Rookwood Red. Remove any remaining graphite carefully with a Magic Rub eraser or with turpentine on a paper towel. Spray lightly with Krylon Matte Spray. Mix an antiquing glaze of turpentine and Burnt Umber oil paint in a Styrofoam tray with a palette knife. The antiquing should be dark but easy to spread. Apply the antiquing to the top of the lamp with a sponge brush, and then lay a sheet of bubble wrap over the antiquing and press evenly all over. Carefully remove the bubble wrap. If the design runs together, the mix is too thin. Repeat on the outer edges of the lamp base. If the antiquing runs into an area where you don't want it, simply wipe off any excess antiquing with turpentine on a paper towel wrapped around your finger. Allow the glaze to dry at least two days. Transfer the pattern for the lettering with white graphite. Base the lettering with a liner or small round brush, using Hauser Medium Green. Shade the bottom of the letters with Dark Forest Green, and highlight the top of the letters with Hauser Light Green. Shade below the letters with a mixture of 1 part Rookwood Red + 1 part Black. Varnish and enjoy!

Base the lettering with a liner or a no. 2 round. It's better if you can completely cover the graphite.

Shade the bottom of each letter and highlight the top with a no. 2 flat. Shade below the lettering with a no. 4 flat.

INDEX